SELECTED, NEW, AND UNPUBLISHE 1980-2(

MERVYN LINFORD

THE LITTORAL PRESS

First published in 2006
by The Littoral Press
10 Prail Court, Vesta Close
Coggeshall, Essex CO6 1QG

13 digit: ISBN 978-0-9550926-4-0
10 digit: ISBN 0-9550926-4-7

© Mervyn Linford 2006

British Library Cataloguing-in-Publication Data:
A catalogue record of this book is available from the
British Library

All rights reserved

Printed and bound in Great Britain by
4edge Ltd, Hockley. www.4edge.co.uk

Acknowledgements

Mervyn Linford's poetry has appeared in many magazines and periodicals including: Acumen, A Bard Hair Day, Candelabrum, The Countryman, Earth Love, ImageNation, The Independent, Iota, The London Magazine, Orbis, Ore, Outposts, Peace and Freedom, Pentacle, The Poetry Church, Poetry Cornwall, Poetry Monthly, P.N.Review, The Poet Tree, Romantic Renaissance, Rubies in the Darkness, Seam, Sol, Southend Poetry, Staple and Wayfarers.

POETRY COLLECTIONS BY THE AUTHOR:

'Nevertheless through Grasses' (in 'Two Essex Poets' with Frederic Vanson) The Brentham Press 1993

'Talking to the Bees' - The Brentham Press 1997

'Autumn Manuscript' - The Littoral Press 2001

'The Beatitudes of Silence' - The Littoral Press 2003

'Double Vision' (with Clare Harvey) The Littoral Press 2005

'The Wheel of Weathers' - The Littoral Press 2006

FOREWORD

What follows is written more by the way of an apologia than is usual for a foreword in a book of poetry. Over the years I have written poems on a wide variety of subjects but more often than not my work concerns itself with nature, and more latterly, spirituality. Poets of nature and/or spirituality are often criticised nowadays for writing work that has little or no contemporary relevance. In one rejection slip from an editor of a well known poetry magazine I was told: 'But I wish you'd give nature a rest and write about something else. You have expressive talent. But find a theme with more blood in it'. 'Red in tooth and claw' perhaps! A good poem is a good poem no matter what the subject matter and I for one am happy to read work on just about any theme. Unfortunately, many magazine editors and poetry publishers seem to have a blind spot where the poetry of nature and the spirit is concerned. That is one of the main reasons why I started the Littoral Press. I wanted to help poets of merit, who wrote about the aforementioned subject matter, get their work into the public domain. Getting a collection published is not easy at the best of times but in this somewhat materialistic age if you write about 'god' or the natural environment it is even harder.

My spiritual affiliations range between a symbolic interpretation of Christianity and a more eclectic form of paganism. I believe, as many spiritual masters have taught, that all is one and that what we perceive as reality is in fact the multifaceted manifestation of an infinite thought or idea. What interests and inspires me to write is the way I/we relate as a thinking and sentient part of the natural environment. The cycles of the seasons, the cycles of our lives, and their correspondences. The environment and spirituality are in fact one and the same thing. How we relate to 'god', nature and each other is fundamentally a matter of the spirit - if you'll excuse the seeming contradiction in terms! As far as I'm concerned all is metaphor; extrapolated from the infinite 'thought' through nature and ultimately into us as human beings. Our primal relationship is the one we have with 'Mother Earth'. Unless we get that right all other relationships will cease to exist altogether. I and others of like mind try in our own ways to promote the noble, spiritual and creative side of humanity and hope, that even if only in a small way, we can help to counteract some of the dark, ignoble and destructive traits of our ever-increasing species. To love 'god', our neighbours, and have a true reverence for the natural world is as far as I'm concerned of the most crucial contemporary relevance.

When I was a child I lived in Pitsea in Essex which was then in the early fifties just a small marshland village waiting to be subsumed by Basildon New Town. In 1969 I felt that my childhood was being covered in brick and concrete and consequently desired a change of scenery. Unfortunately, I couldn't afford to move back into the country to experience the wonders of nature as I had as a young child so I decided to move into rented accommodation in Southend-on-Sea. At least there I would have the mudflats and the wildfowl and waders to interest and inspire me. When I reached 60 years of age I was in the position where I could apply for sheltered accommodation. I have now managed to re-establish myself in the village of Coggeshall in north Essex so I'm back in the sort of environment where I started as a child. The village is literally islanded in the countryside. Colchester is eleven miles to the east, Braintree six miles to the west, Kelvedon three miles south and Earls Colne four miles north. I feel as though I can now end my life as it started: closer to the rhythms of the earth and its seasons, more fully attuned to whatever underlying reality we chose to immortalise with the name of 'god' or infinite potentiality.

May all those who read this selected works experience something of Louis MacNeice's 'The drunkenness of things being various'. It is said that 'truth is stranger than fiction'; well in my opinion reality as we perceive it is the strangest thing of all. When we remember what and who we really are, then life partakes fully of the magic and the mystery written in the fields and woods, the marshes and seascapes, and all the suhshot skies and starlit, moon-glorious nights of our infinite and shared existence.

Mervyn Linford
Coggeshall -Essex
October 2007

CONTENTS

POEMS: 1980-1985

Glove Puppets	17
Stranger	18
Icy Whisper	19
And so we Walk	20
Shelter	21
Lapwings	22
Glaucous Gold	23
Beachy Head	24
The Legacy of Moment	25
Hopkinesque	26
Market Labourer	27
Isms and Ologies	28
Crone	29
Dusk over Abberton	30
Moon over Stained Glass	30
The Wheel of Weathers	31
Rising Sap	32
Icescape	33
Autumnal	34
Worm	34
Lions and Lambs	35
Eye Wash	35
Below the Bridge	36
Loose Change	36
Norfolk Broads	37
A Grey Infinity	38
'Guards up an' at 'em'	39
Three Mills at Battlesbridge	40
Notions of the Dispossessed	41
Essex Saltings	42
Unloading Cockles (Leigh-on-Sea)	43
Cutting	44
Tollesbury Marshes	45
Foulness	47
The Whispering of Twice	48
Phoenix	50
Un-creation	51
Cover	51
Flyways	52

Summoned	53
Fox	54
Common Mallow	55
The Bunting Only	56
Servants to the Part	57
The Dying Metaphor	58
Oceanic	58
Pilgrimage	59
Harvest Evensong	60
Communion	60
Walking Away	61
Unconscious of the Trade	61
Metamorphosis	62
Non Compos Mentis	62
Fingers of Rime	63
Snowsearch	63
Great Diving Beetle	64
December Dusk	65
Ship's Cat	66
Holophrastic	67
Widow	68
Days	68
Double Vision	69
Suddenly	70
Blow Out	71
All Flesh is Grass - Mow down a Vegetarian	72
Gardener	73
Derivative (Beeleigh Essex)	74
January Dusk	75
September Morning	75
Argument in Autumn	76
Playground	76
Summer Storm	77
Fly	78
A Rich Preserve	79
River Album	79
Captain	80
On the Verge	81

POEMS: 1986-1990

Midnight	82
A Silent Understanding	82

To Staunch a Wound	82
Hic Transit Gloria Mundi	83
Clifftown	83
Billingsgate	84
Spring Flower	84
Blackbird	85
Tracks	85
Elim Lil	86
Grandmother	87
Bird Nesting	88
Amazonian Clone Parable	89
Beanflowers	90
A Question of Bridges	91
Weirpool	92
Watercolour	93
Spell	94
Timepiece	95
Closing the Till	96
Kingfisher	97
Sailing Barges	97
Lachryma Christi	98
Easterly	99
Night Watch	99
Demystified	100
Mehalah's Isle	100
Plotlands	101
Resurrection	102
Compulsary Purchase	103
Holy Week	104
February	105
White Light	105
August Bank Holiday	106
A Sad Expression	106
Cuckoo Land	107
Agnostic	107
April the First	108
The Esoteric Angler	109
The Treatment	110
Hedgehog Pie	111
New Town	112
Walking Ganger	114
Cultivation	115
Landing	115

Twitcher	116
Heavenwards	117
Stanley Road	118
Handing in the Keys	119
Parks and Gardens	120
Robin	120
Bird Watching	121
Testing the Water	121
May the Fifth	122
Summer Night	123
Watching Swallows	123
Caterpillars	124
On Line	124
February the Twenty Ninth	125
Ritualistic	127
Journeys	128
Middle Age	129
Water-splash	130
Young Barn Owls	131
Bellbine	132
Fox Cub	133
Matinee	133
Hunters	134
St Benet's Sheep	135
Ulting Church	135
December Hunt	136
Challenge	137
Late September	137
Game's Master	138
Grandfather	139
Extra! Extra!	140
Violets	141
Gathering Holly	142
Wilderness	142
Great Tit	143
The Sawyer's Tale	144
Chelmer Valley	146
Starling	147
The Back Path	148
Cat	148
Canada Geese	149
The Falconer	149
Crocuses	150

Coincidence	150
Homesteader	151
Blank	152
Song	153
Late March	153
In the Woods	154
Changeable	155
On Days	155
Spring Hatch	156
Double Take	156
Cricket Bat Willows	157
Once	157
Words for Autumn	158
Fog	158
Willow Cutting	159
Moments	160

POEMS: 1991-1995

Death Slide	165
Spirits	166
Windy Day	166
Snow Piece	167
A Day in March	167
New Moon	167
Barn Owl	168
Turbulence	168
Song Thrush	169
March Morning	169
Singularity	170
Talking to the Bees	171
Nevertheless through Grasses	172
Humbug	173
Jackson's Pond	174
Plotlanders	175
Casualty	176
Genesis	177
Unrequited	178
Rough Grained	179
Changing Tense	180
Some Hope	181
Rella's	182
Chapter and Verse	183

Early Chapter	184
Learning the Tricks	185
Cheers!	186
Topsy Turvy	187
In Arrears	189
Being Original	191
A Swinging Mood	192
Fuming	193
Luxembourg	194
Sacrifice	195
Precinct	196
Party Political Broadcast circa 1492	197
Pithecanthropus	198
Watching the Game	199
Bypassed	200
Black Coffee	201
Small Boats (Leigh-on-Sea)	202
Crystal Gazing	202
"Nice Weather we're Having"	203
Pigeon Post	204
Summer Deep	205
Red Herring	205
May Day	206
A Lark in Summer	206
Clods	207
End of Season	208
Ardrossan to Brodick	208
Circus	209
First Impressions	210
Autumn Forecast	210
Through a Glass Brightly	211
All Saints	212
South Downs	212
Eastbourne Pier	213
Hanningfield Reservoir	213
Misnomer	214
Churchend Paglesham	214
Meridian	215
Song at Dusk	215
Woodham Ferrers	215
Passing Summer	216
Bridal	217
Gargoyles	218

Moon	218
Suburbia	219
Reflections	219
Transported	220
Autumn Woods	220
Guy Fawkes	221
Autumn Blackbirds	222

POEMS; 1996-2000

Noah's Wife	223
After Freezing Fog	224
Brent Geese	225
Fog	225
Seagull	226
Ulting Church	226
Journey Home	227
Detonation	228
Fields of Rape	229
Spring	230
December Rain	231
Christmas Eve	233
Countdown to Midnight	234
February Blizzard	236
Starling Roost	237
Gang	238
Take Over	239
St Peters Paglesham	240
October Mist	241
April Swallows	242
Heat Wave	242
Ramsons	243
Adeste Fideles	244
A Moonless Equilibrium	245
Acquittal	245
Garden Party	246
Golden Harvest	247
Mucking (Essex)	248
The Immemorial Elms	249
Remaindered	250
I.M. Elizza Gozzet	251
Autumn Manuscript	252

POEMS: 2001-2006

Anonymous	253
Lost	253
Chemotherapy	254
Green Woodpecker	255
Southchurch Hall	256
Long-tailed Tits	257
The Green Man	257
Harmonic	258
Atmospheric	259
Monumental	259
Metamorphoses	260
March Snow	261
Shelter	262
A Bee in October	263
The Robin and the Wren	264
Weeping Cherry	265
Snare	266
Leaves	267
Dryads	268
The Light Beyond	269
Semblance	270
Travellers	270
Fiction (for Wallace Stevens)	271
John Barleycorn	271
Honey (for Rupert Brooke)	272
Mute Swans	272
The Beatitudes of Silence	273
Gods	273
Black-Bird	274
Sun-Struck	274
The Church of Leaves	275
Toadstools	276
The Lark Ascending	277
All Saints	278
Bucks Cross Cottage	279
Beetles	280
Connections	280
Shield Bugs	281
By the River	281
In the Bud	282
Cold text - Warm Collation	283

Mirage	284
River Thurne	285
Snowdrops by the River	286
Song of Ourselves	287
Stasis	288
Songs of Light	289
I	290
January the Seventeenth	291
The Rose and the Nightingale	291
Revelations	292
Silver Shadows	293
Apparently	294
Chill Breath	295
Asymmetry	296
Daffodils	297
Skylark	298
A Song for Easter	299
The Litany of Summer	299
Swan Lake	300
Sunlight and Celandine	301
Sound and Silence	302
Blue Eyes at Eastertide	302
The Heart's Investment	303
Depths of Blue	304
Tadpoles	305
The Blossoming of Death (for Christina Rossetti)	305
Reprise	306
Cadences	307
Love Songs and Syringa	308
If	309
Can it be Said?	310
Phased by Moonlight	311
Whit-out at Barling Magna	312
Ice and the Evening Star	313
February Thrush	314
Signs	314
Zero and Below	315
Spoken	316
Melting Snow	317
Sundial	318
Beyond the Glare	319
January Fog	320
Underground Movement	321

After the Rain	322
Summers End	323
Crock of Gold	324
December the 27th	324
December Dusk	325
Patio Window	326
Ingatestone - Essex	327
Basis	328
Summer River	328
Winter Berries - Spring Flowers	329
Trinity	329
May	330
Otters	331
Blossom Time	332
Wrens and Roses	333
Collared Doves	334
Do not Despair	335
Mirror Image	336
A Lack of Symbols	337
Snow and Shadows	338
A Temporal Arrangement	338
A Rose for Sirius	339
Doves and Darkness	340
Union	341
Tidal	342
The Skylark's Golden Song	343
Mistletoe and Ivy	344
Simple Things	345
Green Plovers	346
Curlew and Cumuli	347
Lion House	348
Innocence Regained	349
Slasher Martin	350
The Nightingale and the Rose	351
Frozen	352
Bream	353
Snowy Woods	354
Adlestrop or Ulting?	355
Enlightened	356
The Battle of Ashingdon	357
Migrations	358
'Beeing'	359
A Word about Snow	360

Optical	361
'Blackthorn Winter'	362
Conversing with Snowdrops	363
Gold Rush	364
Larksong and Leaf-Fall	365
Woodland Ride	366
The Way it is	367
New Year's Day	368
Blackbird and Blossom	369
Hadleigh Ray	370
Turnstones	371
Reflections - Sugar Mill Cottages (Hoe Mill - Essex)	372
Dreams of Fish and Other Forms	373
All is Now	375
I See the Snow	376
Another Light	377
Silences and Sound	378
As Above	379
Fields of Vision	380
Slack Water	381
River Triptych	382
Heaven and Hell	384
The Bure Marshes (Norfolk)	385
Reprise	386
The Season Burns	387
Star Gazing	388
Perhaps I'm Wrong	389
Passing Images	389
The Tragedy of Love	390
Skylarks and Cumuli	391
The Shivering Stars	391
Reasonable Things	391
The Snow Falls	392
Whispering Swans	392
Falling Leaves	392
The Trouble was he Battled with the Stars	393
Summer Rain	394
'Can Spring be far Behind'	395
The Saxon Shore	396
A Dalliance with Rainbows	397
St Peter's Chapel	398
A Man in the Park	399
Sirius Singing	400

1980 – 1985

GLOVE PUPPETS

Hey you up there, you with decision
   At ethereal fingertips;
Could you not slip us the wink,
Drop a few hints on immortality?

Not that I think you mean with your truths,
I've seen the signs, the ritual portents
Handed down with a pious solemnity.

I can excuse you the masterful game
Pulling our strings with your knotted secrets;
But not the rest of the tricksters
Sticking their mitts into all our yearnings.

STRANGER

I'm always there
Crouching unseen in sly corners
Waiting to pounce on the unsuspecting.

I'm not an image found in the frame
Of recurring dreams; nor a steady focus
Sharpened by words across the mind's screen.

I'm a vague, amorphous force, a faceless,
Thoughtless, shiver of nothingness;
A rattle at the heart's cage, a knot of sinew
Bunching the blood in the stomach's prison -

The hammer of unthinking moments
Driving its nails through the lid of consciousness.

ICY WHISPER

I can feel the weight
Of winter in the sun
Casting its low light
Across golden fields.

The harvest over and
The plover-flustered skies,
Finches flock-happy
On fallen grain
And the starling dusk
Shedding the first
Of autumn's leaves.

The final flurry
Of a fruitful season:
Hurrying shades
Of loaded trailers
Moon high
With winter bedding –

Voices behind cocked guns
And the strung death
Of thresh-scattered rabbits.

An early owl
Pampers the gloom
On hushed wings
And the lunar palm
Is crossed by a skein
Of northern silver.

AND SO WE WALK

And so we walk and we see the world
Or the world as we wish to see it.

A low sea wall wearies its way
Between the April light, to where the quick sun
Fractures its face on a slow, grey tide.

A curlew flutes and its liquid notes
Ghost across salt-blue skies
To where horizons are the land's lip
And time but a thought in which we wander.

And so we walk and we see the world
Or the world as we wish to see it;
Where the year's first fluster their wings
Around a lion's tooth, and transience
    Is a fresh collection
Pinned under glass by the point of spring.

Lion's tooth: dent de lion – dandelion.

SHELTER

Prying with eyes
Or snout-wise into every crevice,
Nevis's of huge thought
Sunning their slopes
Under measured skies.

Study the slugs
Under phantom shells
Munching their diet
Out of Eden's greenery.

Will it safely under blue tomorrows
Or loudly where the swallow feeds the sun?

Window me back from the falling rain,
Machine me from the blinding storm,
Wheel me on wheels across your vast mechanics.

Manufacture me my last delights,
My nights of owls on tensile springs,
My days of wings - delta on ballistic hawks.

Spill me the brains brimming in the blackest sump
And carry the crater from its waiting moon.

Rocket me on wasted limbs
To where gravity no longer mocks
And the star's long blood
Trickles its planets through un-peopled veins -

Read me where the eyes fold back,
Filling their wisdom with unwritten tears.

LAPWINGS

Sometimes, when spring, like a green idea
Dispenses with winter and its icy reason -
When the season's instinct
Proffers a flower to enamoured bees
And leaves between showers
Whisper their secrets to flirtatious light:

Then may you see them on the skittish air,
Those careless plovers
Cresting their passion on erratic wings -
High, in their raptures of rhapsodic flight
As they climb, but to tumble
From the sun's seduction;

Then may you see them in the wind's embrace
As they cry, like derision
Over jilted pasture -
Where the sky, made frantic
By their fleet attention,
Clings, like a lover, to each thin proposal.

GLAUCOUS GOLD

There is a land that has a Saxon heart
Where language of the Latinate is least,
Where Nordic on a tongue of salt is cast
On level lines towards the northern seas.
And there am I, a pilgrim on the shore,
Abandoned by the stars that were my home
To form or fail, by what unwritten law
That leaves a man such solitudes to roam?
This ooze, that in the miracle of light
Can seem as though eternity in time,
Will sudden turn to dark on lowering sky
And leave the soul, so desolate, so blind.
And yet, these bleak horizons hold me still,
No risen scarp can move my leaden faith;
No undulating wealth of upland fields
Could buy the rich seclusion of this place.
This glaucous gold is all that I could wish,
The spirit's voice on skeins of endless geese;
Alluvial, the though that through the mist
Attaches shape to solitary trees.
So here I wait the memory of tides
Where curlew call like echoes of the past
And over top the heron ghostly glides
Across the wide and moon-suffusive marsh.

BEACHY HEAD

This cliff has become a tourist attraction -
Not just for the lighthouse down below,
Or the chalk-blue sea, swirling over white rocks;

Not for the monkshood or the viper's bugloss,
Not even for the purple thyme
Spreading its carpet at the foot of summer.

No-one watches the falcons;
Borne on the up-draught of a warming wind -
Touching their talons in pretend exchanges.

The clue is in the notice on the wall -
Nothing subtle, just ring the Samaritans,
It's never too late, we're always there.

So it's here that we test ourselves;
Teeter on the edge, stare down the sheer face -
Are frightened by our own imaginations.

What would it be like, to fly like a jackdaw,
A black speck, curving on the salt air -
Feeling the thermals in the width of pinions?

We'll never know, our kind is heavy;
We gravitate on darkness and despair -
The pull of tides, the moon's psychotic phases.

THE LEGACY OF MOMENT

To touch the note that pitches to emotion
And shatter once the spirit's vibrant glass,
To pass beyond the singing of devotions
And ring as with the frequency of stars.

What more to ask, than some eternal notion
Should make its claim on secular ideas,
Should soothe as balm, a universal potion
And turn to light the undiscerning tear.

To hear as if the intellectual quotient
Was balanced by an infinite design,
A paradigm, like waves upon an ocean
That crest but once, contented to decline.

To taste upon the lips of my atonement
The living blood, a dark fermenting wine,
That takes from life the legacy of moment
And leaves to death the sediments of time.

HOPKINESQUE

How the fish leap -
How the rings round, gold, and concentric,
Preach of perfection in the hush of alders.

How the wing, wet, heaves from its hatching
   to the weather's web -
Dances and dapples in the dawn, silk, silent.

Look to the wind's paw -
   the cat, quick,
Claw on the water in a raft of ripples.

What is it -
What in the air's arc
Visits like velvet to the once reflections?

Why in the cloud, clear,
Does the sun's glance
Dash to a dazzle in a frame of fragments?

Ah how the eye weeps -
How the known deep, cowers and closes
Through a glass that's broken.

Look to the self, shape -
   to the bone, break,
Quarrel and quiver in the delve that doubles.

Know in the light's lens,
   how the bow, bend,
Rights its refraction to the soul's meniscus.

See as the wind wanes,
How the heart's hope
Shivers and settles to a lucid image.

MARKET LABOURER

Why do they laugh at me, I do no wrong?
I always sweep the market till it's clean -
Run errands for their sandwiches and tea
And sing my songs to please and entertain them.
I am a man who always tries to please -
Perhaps my words belong on younger lips,
But can I help my lack of education?
I want to learn, yet cannot quite remember -
And yet I'm strong; I help them to unload
Their vans, set out the stalls with all they need,
And smile when they think it's fun to goad me.
I do not understand, my face is red,
My hands are fat, my fingers thick and round.
I am so tall I cannot help but stoop
Instead of walking proudly, like a soldier.
I am a fool, but even fools need love -
Why is the world made lonely by their laughter.

ISMS AND OLOGIES

Isms and ologies where are you now,
Now that my tenant is love -
Isms and ologies send my apologies
I'm in the hands of the dove.

I am above you, have suffered and snubbed you,
Mine are the wings of the free –
Isms and ologies send my apologies
I'm climbing back up the tree.

You take the light in the lamp of ecologies,
You take the road of the apes -
But goad me no more with your laws and economies,
Feed me the opulent grapes.

Isms and ologies, prisons and solitaries,
Sever the cerebral chains –
Wake me no more with the mist of idolatries,
Waive your material claims.

I must away from your terrible qualities,
Values and voice of the just –
Isms and ologies send my apologies,
Time has no room on the bus.

CRONE

Like a spider in its lair that waits
Foot-sensitive to sound's vibration,
Down by the door she hangs her threads
To lure the silk of conversation.

The lightest tread will spring the trap,
Good morning drips from poison fangs -
The quick escape is deftly wrapped,
The invitation dangles.

And there inside that dark deceit,
The chitin crisp of empty shells -
She sucks her fill until replete,
On scandal's breath she swells.

She drains the kindness out of speech,
Her spinneret shot through with lies -
An insect in an insect's niche,
A calumny with smiles.

DUSK OVER ABBERTON

The sun like a molten seal
Buries its wax
Into night's long charter.

Paragraphs of low light
Section the sky
In vermillion tones.

Terminal dots of rooks and daws
Hurry the day
Through its punctuation;

And a signature of seven swans
Witness the velum,
Making dusk official.

MOON OVER STAINED GLASS

Movements of a moonlit night,
Shattered into stained-glass images.

Reflections, perhaps, of religious purpose,
Or refractions of a longed for light
Scattered in fragments by a lead-locked vision.

THE WHEEL OF WEATHERS

Times have I witnessed
On their course unbending:
Soft summer words
In whisperings of light
Weaving their language
Through the silent meadows -

Have seen such seasons
With the heart's perception
Where dreams are written
Into living chapters.

Times have I listened
To the tearful voices:
To the hours turning
On the wheel of weathers,
Where leaves are worried
Into sweeps of sadness
And the harvest darkens
Into burnt Septembers.

Times I remember
When the stars were flowers:
When the frozen heavens
Showered their petals
In a fleece of crystal
And the twisted branches
Shone with the sparkle
Of immense beginnings.

Times I have travelled
To the birth of ages:
To the cold contraction
Of the earth's insistence -
Where the day is woken
To a winter's weeping
And the sun's warm fingers
Cling to the sepals
Of the clay's creation.

RISING SAP

See how the *orchis* swells with spring -
How the hare boxes over breasts of hills
Adding momentum to the growing lust.

See how the flower spreads its lips -
How the year's first phallus
Hovers on the scent of sex.

Observe the passion in the land's warm juices:
The darting tongues of erotic fish -
And the frog's blank wisdom
Arming its urges with instinctive claws.

Notice the sea over rhythmic knees
Lifting its buttocks to the moon's alignment -
And the tree's long fingers,
Teasing the breath from the sun's coy migraine.

ICESCAPE

Snow, like the lolling of suspended tongues
Laps into layers over hedge and bank.

Fields are skivvied into sweeps of green
As a besom wind bristles through the winter wheat.

Blizzards of beleaguered rooks
Blow black and buoyant through the swirl of air
And the sun's low orbit
Slips into shivers through the frozen dusk.

Willows whistle at the river's edge -
Their cold, stark limbs
Locked in a prison of translucent ice.

The season slithers on the snap of frost
And the slow, dark fish
Glide through the strata's of a zero aspic.

AUTUMNAL

September stills
And all in limbo hangs.

The tide turns
Its metaphor to glass
And the wide zostera
Glistens with greenness
In the misted light.

Scraps of discarded paper
Flap into focus
And revert to gulls -

Glide into greyness
And are lost forever.

The weather's breath
Pivots on the season's edge -
Exhales into autumn
On a skein of whispers.

WORM

Tomorrow I turn, learn new tricks,
Angle reason for its ganglion answer.

The nerve's edge, nudges, into nebulosity -
Picks up space, touches light, insinuates form.

Material is manifest - captures the vacuum:
The cerebral cortex, covets, its conceptual prize -
Imagines galaxies, creates infinity, names its relationships.

LIONS AND LAMBS

The high elms snap wood
Against the March wind.

Elated rooks race and revel
In their spring debate.

A prowl of cloud
Rages in ferocious skies -

And the timid fields
Chase through the shadows
On a bleat of flowers.

EYE-WASH

What is an eye but the nerve's wish:
   A glass-blown fish
Swimming in a sea of light -
The brain's need splitting the sky
Into wisdom's rainbow?

What is an eye but the body's must -
   The blood's weak hand
Guiding the blind into total darkness?
What is an eye but the heat of stars -
   Or the earth's cold crust
Let as a tear from the cosmic carcass?

BELOW THE BRIDGE

Follow the fish in their bright shoals:
See how they swim as one -
How the sun's face mirrors their every move.

Observe that they know their place -
That not thought or the waste of words
Alters their silver symmetry.

Take notes, innately if you can:
Study the snap of a moment's fear -
    How in death's gaze
Shape is the scatter of survival's art.

Then relate in reason how the fragments close -
    How the storm's dross
Blends into silence and concentric calm.

LOOSE CHANGE

The snow came fitfully at first -
Its thin commitment
Minted in whiteness
Like a winter's coinage.

Intermittent bursts
Of loose change
Flipping and falling
On the toss of air;

As if the sky's investment
Held but a pittance
For the child's interest.

NORFOLK BROADS

I know a stretch of water
Where the wild English rose
Tumbles free between the alder and the ash -
Where the lily floats a flower
As the river slowly flows
Over silver-sided fish that brightly flash.

Where the reeds forever answer
To the quest of every breeze
With a whisper through the wilderness of green -
And the fields of golden harvest
Glister far beneath the leaves
Under skies that smoke a misted blue between.

A level land that widens
Past the windmill and the staithe
To an island's height of isolated oaks -
Where the church abuts a tower
To the tides of northern grey
As they sough to white in waves along the coast.

I know a stretch of water
That's a mirror to the sloop
As it sails towards an erubescent sun -
Where the wings of dusk are falling
Through the light in listing loops
And the night exhales the breath that day begun.

A GREY INFINITY

Not a sun-crest wave
Breaks on the ocean
Of this cold October.

Hills of mist
Climb ever cloud-ward
Into muted vision.

Hedges - more blue than green -
Narrow perspective
To a grey infinity.

Furrows of rich, brown earth
Roll - like a seascape -
Into ebbs of light;

And the slow, dark birds
Fade - like flotillas -
Over still horizons.

'GUARDS, UP AN' AT 'EM'

By Jackson's farm the centuries evolve:
The yeoman's house, its cottages and barns -
A church that crowns what Essex calls a hill
And far around the fields and shining furrows.
The chestnut trees are yellowing to brown -
Their fallen leaves, like hands across the pond
That drift and drown with white-forgotten feathers.
The graveyard, all but silent, save the sounds
Of starlings as they settle to their roost;
And by the porch an epitaph that's proud
For one 'John Cole' who fought at Waterloo -
Who wounded then, would still be wounded now,
If he arose with medals on his chest
To hear the distant barrage of the traffic.

THREE MILLS AT BATTLESBRIDGE

Here, the confluence of centuries -
   three mills -
Three histories of quern and staple
Ground from their meaning by the tides of traffic.

One whose wheels were overshot by time -
Now but the grist for powder-paint and palette.

   Three mills -
Three moments in the mystery of grain -
Steeped in the engine of revolving light.

One who knew of vacuum and steam -
Of spritsails that are ghosted by the quay.

Here, the confluence of centuries -
   three mills -
Three entries in the register of man
Bound to the landscape by the chaff of seasons.

The last a husk of broken steel and weeds -
Now obsolete in dust and dereliction.

NOTIONS OF THE DISPOSSESSED

They came unwelcome
To the house of plenty -
Their tongues a tangent
To the level voices.

We knew the stricture
In their sharp phonetics -
The harsh arena
Of their accusation.

Theirs was no lesson
In absurd semantics -
No pious cryptic
Coined by the wordy
From a bankrupt language.

We had our answers:
Our parameters of thought -
Our own compartments
Of articulation.

We saw no purpose
In their hieroglyphics -
Their weight of meaning
Resting its burden
On our glib achievements.

ESSEX SALTINGS

First time for decades
   they say –
Ice in great white
   plates
Turning the saltings
Into thoughts of tundra.

Memories of past
   millennia –
Of lands created
At the frozen edge.

The teal cut coldly
On a wedge of wings –
Burning the substance
Of their own survival.

A thought swings
   northwards
Through a nerve of air –
Touching the sinews
Of another age.

Notions of despairing
   tribes
Skirting the limits
Of a vast moraine,

With the far blue
   distance
Carved by serrations
Into slope and summit.

A curlew flutes
Its glacial refrain
And time's slow music
Melts to the moment
And the mind's erosion.

UNLOADING COCKLES (LEIGH-ON-SEA)

The cockle fleet uplifts the artist's thumb
And frames itself in old-world atmospherics.
The sun loads light across the creek
   And girls with skin like umber
Tease their impressions in a swirl of pastel.
We read the signs that vie for evocation:
      'Peter Boat' and 'Smack'
      'Old Ship' and 'Crooked Billet'.
Along the streets and cobble-dinted lanes
      Shadows from houses
Angle like easels in a clash of contrast.
      The sea beyond
Scumbles the skyline into blue opaquely –
Blurs into billows of diminished ochre.
   A man with a heavy yoke
Changes perspective, like a print that's faded –
Carries the burden of intense nostalgia.

CUTTING

How we loved that embankment -
To clamber through the hot, oppressive air,
Logging the numbers of the selfsame engines.

To lie contented in the grass -
Those bread and sugar hours,
With the great moon daisies

Nodding above us with an eye for insects.
There we would place our pennies on the track -
Heady with mischief

And the whiff of danger.
The smell of coal and tar -
Thick and pervasive in a glaze of light.

The whir of wires through rings and pulleys,
As the shifting signals
Clattered their message on the tilt of iron.

So far away, those ant-infested slopes -
Lizards and slowworms
Evasive with the loss of tails;

The passengers with time enough to wave
And the steam's dank texture,
Cool and condensing, like the bloom on damsons.

TOLLESBURY MARSHES

Down on Tollesbury marshes
That is where I wish to be
Where the purslane and the grasses
Meet the high-roads of the sea –
Where the bees across the saltings
Feed on lavender and light
And the barley, ripe for malting,
Climbs the camber of the dykes.

Where the butterflies are brimming
On the bounty of the hedge,
Through the golden air are swimming
Over thistledown and sedge –
Like a carnival that clamours
Through the cavalcade of days
Every colour's wing a banner
On the brine be-dazzled haze.

Down on Tollesbury marshes
That is where I wish to be
Where each hour's breath that passes
Is as listless as the breeze –
Where the flowers flood forever
Through the ways that wend and fetch
Like a viper's slow endeavour
Through the many-purpled vetch.

Where the blue is ever wider
Than the sun is summer high
And the silken threaded spiders
Trace the currents of the sky –
Where the gossamer that glistens
Is the glint on herons' wings
And the linnet looks and listens
As the yellowhammer sings.

Down on Tollesbury marshes
By the high-roads of the sea
Where the purslane meets the grasses
That is where I wish to be –
Where the web of light is wefted
Through the water's woven loom
And each shadow's weight is hefted
By the feather's breath of noon.

FOULNESS

Give me the sway of the sibilant reeds
And the sweep of ebullient sky
Where the shadows that run
In their race with the sun
Are as fleet as the showers that sigh;
Where horizons are wide
To the surge of the tides
And the dykes are reticular gold,
Where the scent on the breeze
Is the salt of the sea
And the surf turns to wheat as it rolls.

Give me the air where the harrier wings
Over levels of turbulent grass,
Where the lilt of the lark in cerulean rings
And the wind is the voice of the marsh;
Where the ways are as few
As the trees they eschew
Save the elms that encircle the farms,
Where the mews overtop
In ubiquitous flocks
And the owl haunts the loft and the barn.

Give me the space where the wires relate
Like the strings of Aeolian harps,
Where the tales that are told
Like the sagas of old
Are the warp and the weft of the heart;
Where the shivering coast
Hangs the breath of a ghost
Over waves in a whisper of white
And returns to the land
Its enveloping hand
Through the sleeve of unspeakable night.

THE WHISPERING OF TWICE

If you should go to Baddow
By the mill pond and the weir
When the autumn winds are ploughing from the west;
When the clouds draw out their furrows
And the trees are all but bare
Save the high sporadic tangle of a nest.
You will see the river rising
Through the brown-bedraggled reeds
Till it spills across the meadows like a shroud;
See the plovers dip and diving
With an air-enacted ease
As the weather whets the edge of every sound.

If you should go to Baddow
When the year is at the turn
And the bridge a slip of black-deceptive ice;
Where the ghost of every willow
Is a spectre in reverse
And the world becomes the whispering of twice;
You will see the rime evolving
From an insubstantial mist –
Like a memory that manifests in white;
Every fern of frost extolling
What the mind would yet resist
If allowed the sharp lucidity of light.

If you should go to Baddow
When the equinox is near
And the night a perfect echo to the sun;
Where the set of every shadow
Is commensurate and clear
With the rising tide of something just begun;
You will see the first expression
Of a sentiment within
As it climbs above the tegument of earth;
See the quill of every question
Fletch a feather to its wings
As it flies above the gravity of birth.

If you should go to Baddow
When the barley stoops with gold
And the swallow scythes the harvest of the air;
When the willow-herb and mallow
Are the promises foretold
And the drone of heat as solemn as a prayer;
You will know beyond reflection
How the season is fulfilled
And the summer's mill exhausted by the grist;
How the moon – its blown perfection –
Like a quern above the hills
Carries dusk towards a cold-forgotten tryst.

PHOENIX

Some other
Language
Is this
Cold
November,
Other
Than
A memory
Of words.
The fire
Burns
Its drift
Of golden
Leaves,
And smoke,
Like slow
Semantics,
Rises
In silence
Through
The mists
Of meaning.

UN-CREATION

Stripping the land of man's investment -
Un-choking in the smokeless skies of imagination.

The worrying down of synthetic structures -
Down to the poison bones of motivation.

Even the church un-bricks its certainties -
Releasing the ground for an earlier magic.

The elimination of fossils
Un-laid forever by receding seas.

The wordless measures of un-historic rock
Locking their light in a crystal cipher.

Then only fragments, an atomic essence
Swirling in search of a new direction -
Waiting its chance to be proved insane.

COVER

What should we here imply:
These headlands so conspicuously left -
Freed from the poison of a growing market.

These edges of agrarian intent
In flower only for the sporting harvest.

The ground on which our platitudes are bred -
Our green excuses, hung like the pheasant
And the dying partridge?

FLYWAYS

What birds tonight are flighting down the lanes -
What slow migration on a stream of wings
Spills from the quiet to an iceless shore?

What moon of thought has carried them afar -
    Like star-lost children
Drawn to the purpose of a dim commitment?

What feather's swim of deep, un-dawning dark
Drifts on the currents of instinctive tides -
Sinks to the sounding of a mute exhaustion?

SUMMONED (I.M. SIR JOHN BETJEMAN)

He dies, an age passes,
And the eye reduces
Metaphor to tears.

Such years that found
Their rhythm in his words,
Fade to the blur
Of a world unrhymed,
And time steers backwards
From its broken metre.

An unclear diction
Moves in discordance
From the ear of music -
Reaches in reason
For its share of knowledge.

The simple heart
Cowers its image
From the lucid line -
Dares not from the darkness
To affirm tradition.

The chime of ages
Passes to the knell of verse,
And the living language
Wilts for the water
In a well immortal.

FOX

Hunter and hunted -
Slinks into sunset
On a thread of shadows.

Clever as a star's wink -
Quick and cunning
Into moons of mischief.

Killer and killed -

Haunter of the field's edge
Spilling from hawthorn
Into screams of darkness.

Redder than the rill of carnage -
Saunters through silver
With a shock of feathers.

COMMON MALLOW

The mallow speaks
Indelibly of June -
Tells more to me
Of heavy-scented days
Than any song.

Hirsute in throngs
Of purple-headed
    flowers
It mentions heat
As soundlessly
    as light.

Belongs indeed
To hours in the sun
Where minutes strung
Like memories extant -
Languish forever in the
Pearl's translucence.

THE BUNTING ONLY

These fields are heavy
With the weight of summer:
The barley yields
On many drooping heads -
Drowsed in the slumber
Of surrounding poppies.

Heat is a riot
Of erratic dust -
An intrusive movement
Borne on the spiral
Of the warming earth.

The clouds climb slowly
Into seething whiteness
And the bunting only
Jangles in silence
From its burning vantage.

SERVANTS TO THE PART

How should I listen to the words between us:
The language of our long-accustomed thoughts -
These words that say so little, yet enough;
Enough at least to show their meagre force?

You speak, as I, a servant to the part,
Each line rehearsed to take the lover's stage -
Such lines, that once, the lyric of the bard
Still turn the tongue, each other to assuage.

No more can I be partner to the plot,
The farce has run its season of renown -
This actor knows the histrionic cost
Of playing his soliloquy aloud.

What once was heard and rounded with applause,
Projects a sigh, and exits, from the boards.

THE DYING METAPHOR

Take, for instance, the swan -
Graceful of course,
Long-necked and broad of wing.

No song to speak of -
Just a soft invective
If at all disturbed.

You would think
If beauty were a word,
That word itself
Would mirror into whiteness -
Would preen to perfection
In its joy reflected;

But no, through us,
It hankers for its name -
Turns God into the
Ravishment of flesh
And sings, once only,
To the dying instant.

OCEANIC

Galleons were the dream -
Not seamen, but circumnavigators.

Men of the sextant and the mind's meridian
Hauling their sheets through the declinations.

Men of the oceanic myth, borne
By the porpoise and the stormy petrel.

Men in the harness of a splicing wind -
Minded to scrimshaw, and the teeth of sharks.

PILGRIMAGE

We travelled east
From citadels of stone
To where the light's
Glint bone, broke from
The suburbs over open fields.

Traces of a thin snow
Powdered the furrows
Of an iron land
And the thorn-dark hedges
Punctured the shadows
With their stars of frost.

We journeyed on
Uncertain of our way -
Not knowing why
We travelled there at all.

We came to the limits
Of our known horizons -
To where the sea's cold silver
Sighed through its sifting
And the sound of geese.

Alone we stood
In solitudes of ice -
The far west woods
Faded with the memory
Of night and the ruined byre
Dim in the dawning
Of a salt-marsh day.

Our only gifts
Were offerings of prayer
And why we prayed
We did not know at all -
But pray we did,
Like children in despair,
And the warm sun woken
Rose to our bidding,
Like a golden wafer.

HARVEST EVENSONG

Turns now the hour
Into summer's ending:

The high, church clock
Tremors on the edge of dusk -

Where the first rung stars
Peal in the pallor
Of descending light.

Cedar and yew kneel
In the chancel
Of the changing wind

And their blue-dark needles
Sing through the sermon
Like a ghostly choir.

COMMUNION

The river curves beside the church,
Winds uncertain, as if to search
The meaning of its way;
The fields slope down and ears of corn
Break new bread, offer as re-born
The sacrament of day.

I taste such light upon my tongue,
Savour the mystery of sun
In eternal darkness;
Wonder at the chalice of my dreams,
How wine, is once, and all between
Is leaning to the west.

WALKING AWAY

It was worth the walk:
Just to be there -
Away from all that's
Talkative and tires -
Like time and space
In diatribes of thought.

To sit beneath the
Silence of the sun
And breathe - like a
   blessing -
The impartial air.

Contented there where
Carelessness abounds
And words, - like linnets -
Fly from the parting
Of astounded lips.

UNCONSCIOUS OF THE TRADE

How tame it seems; remember when the dream
Was still alive, how you and I would talk
Until we tired; would each to each
In innocence avow, our only cause

Was to the other's need. That love itself
Was nourishment enough; enough to feed
Our ravenous desire. What wealth
It seems we've squandered in our time, we breathe

No more the passion of romance, can take,
Nor give, unconscious of the trade, what once
Our hearts were powerless besides. Those days,
Alas, are done; and who in age re-runs

The fashion of a fast-declining youth,
Or learns again, or feels the pain, of truth?

METAMORPHOSIS

Today should be called
   the first:
The promise fulfilled.

The uncertain spring
Bursts from its sepals
Like a trout from water -
Turns grey to golden
With its scintillations.

  Ripples widen
Into shouts of colour:

The sky's dull cloud
Opens like petals
Into blooms of blueness
And the dun's drab season
Sloughs into spinner
And the sun's emergence.

NON COMPOS MENTIS
See them in any park -
In the shady darkness
Walking their worries
Past the flowered borders.

See past the railings
How the traffic hurries -
How another order
Races regardless
On its road to progress.

Notice the faces
In the lake reflected:
Each slow expression
Warped by the ripple
Of neglected hours -

Each once Narcissus
Drowned by the echo
Of a soundless image.

FINGERS OF RIME

How time-deceptive
Is this winter landscape.

Layers of diurnal mist
Float slow and dream-wise
Through a sleep of whispers.

Trees become white shapes:
Feathered and frosted
In the chill of silence -

Like ghosts grown rigid
On the shock of daylight.

Fingers of rime
Bristle from branches
Into dark dimensions

And wings between vision
Are plucked out of minus
Into sudden ice-fall.

SNOWSEARCH

    Like children we were -
Miles in secret to discover whiteness.

We stopped by a river in the drifted snowscape:
Made tracks like music through the muted meadows
And laughed at the lyric of our simple passion -
Saw grass like footnotes in the tufted margins
As hares loped hill-ward into blue-black spinneys.

    Here, it was winter -
Not harsh like iron into ice destructive
But soft and broken into white and water -
The sun in cirrus settled to westward like a fire faded
And our hearts sank homewards into cold compliance.

GREAT DIVING BEETLE

"I've found a beetle," she said,
"I've put it in a jar for you to look at,
   it may be a Colorado."
Colorado it wasn't; not a pond in view
But it paddled in glass like a deep sea turtle.
A gem in a jar - a malachite broach
Edged and transected with translucent topaz.
Its bite can be painful it's said:
A heavy-jawed and voracious insect -
So I lifted it gently by the broad elytra.
The illusion of stone startled from
Its undersides - like a mottled onyx
Cleaved and polished into beige and brown.
The flattened legs rowed against a thin
   resistance
As they searched for the ocean of their
   own environs.
Where should I place it:
This animate jewel lost to the lustre of its
   bright aquatics -
How in the dryness of a drowning light
Can the lone exotic swim to the sanctum of its
   Own existence?

DECEMBER DUSK

Like Christmas lights
The apples on the tree
Shine through the shadows
Of a cold December.

No leaves are left
To gild the brittle air
That weaves its white
In filaments of frost.

Across the lawn
The robin and the thrush
Hop to the borders
Of a frozen larder.

Roses in a pink rush
Flake to the flurry
Of a fragrant snow
And the moon's bare
    bulb
Glows over gardens
Like a naked hope.

SHIP'S CAT

What of the ship's cat?
Sinuous as any -
Slack on the tide's deck,
Coiled and careful
Like the curve of rope.

No lubber - this -
No sea's slope landward
Into licks of silt,
But ribbed to a ripple
Under furls of flesh.

No less alert than
Those upon the shore
Whose claws have fixed
Their bearing to the earth -

As lean as love
The needle of its eye
Sets like a compass
Into nine horizons.

HOLOPHRASTIC

What a pratt of a man -
What a ding-dong
Bats in the belfry
Of his own esteem.

A this, that, no time,
Hatter of a man -
Belling and braying
In his straw fedora.

What a prick-eared
Ass of a man.
Chiming with chatter
Like a clock gone cuckoo.

A tick-tock, main-spring,
Slack of a man,
Late to the platform
Of a line gone loco.

What a no steam, vacuous man,
Ringing like hammers
On a crooked rail.

A once seen, off-track,
Striking the hour
Like a change of moons -
Waxing and waning
In the wind's asylum.

WIDOW

No, she rarely smiles -
Just struggles to forget.

Her eyes, an exequy for love -
Long-written lines of anguish and regret
For all she left unfinished and unsaid.

She moves her tired blood from room to room -
Imagines the companionship that was,
Then curses the untidiness of tears.

How soon a life to memory is swept -
How few the years to cherish what she's lost.

Of passion and of energy bereft
She spits upon the remnants of a cloth
And wrestles with the treachery of dust.

DAYS (I.M. Philip Larkin)

No more toad, no more Whitsun –
The book is closed on social speculation.

The windows now, reflect some other sun:
    no time to wonder in -
No youthful look to relish or regret.

The afternoons have sidled into dusk
And leaves must wake some other world afresh.

For you the light that congregates is done,
   while night, for us,
Comes running through the fields.

DOUBLE VISION

We wait for the signs -
  we must return
To places for returning.

Snowdrop or crocus:
  no great event -
Nothing of a large importance.

We ask their worth -
Say what are these compared
With the achievements
  of invention.

Will birth be more or less:
  evil contained -
Truth made clearer?

We live our guilt's -
Cannot enjoy the promises
  of spring;

Bear full the weight
Unbalance by the mind
And drag our sacks of beauty
  like a burden.

SUDDENLY

All at once it seems -
Bird and beast,
Field and flower.

The air increased
   with scents
And summer sounds
Breathes but a gentle
   breath.

All is abundance
And the hum of wings -
The fly hovers,
The bee delves,
And the bud-scales
   scatter
Like a mimic autumn.

The chiffchaff
Fills the woods
With repetitions
And the stitchwort
   stars
Burst from the darkness
Of a greensward heaven.

   Bluebells
Like a nether sky
Pour from the copses
Into clouds of hawthorn

And the high larks
   singing -
Crown the occasion
With a golden lyric.

BLOW-OUT

A funny bloke is autumn -
A rare old windbag,
All smoke and bluster.

A brown-ale swill of a man
Frowning to furrows
In the dregs of sunlight.

His had his fill of goodness -
Can barely stand,
So heavy with excesses.

Listen to the way he moans -
How the next drawn breath
Whistle and wheezes
On the weight of weather.

See how he staggers
With his load -
How his sack-full swagger
Bellies and buckles
With the heft of plenty.

He knows the score -
Has seen before December's
 brittle ghost,
Hoary and heartless
With a fist of splinters.

Knows well the boast
Of swallows on the wing -
Wefting like shuttles
From the warp of winter.

ALL FLESH IS GRASS - MOW DOWN A VEGETARIAN

We have a wholemeal sensibility -
An organic preference.

My wife is willing, you could say -
Happy with a vegetable existence.

She soaks her pulses well -
Resists the flesh
In favour of the bean.

Sometimes, when in need of roughage,
We test our fibre
To the nerve's last straw -
Take muesli to its limits.

Once, before decaffeinated coffee,
Between t'ai-chi and meditation,
We made a list of our achievements.

She said it was good to be good -
That peas and lentils
Were closer to the gods.

I said that I agreed -
That cows were sacred
And people should be satisfied
    with legumes.

We knew that there was room for all -
That greediness was tantamount to meat
And grass the dilemma of our ruminations.

GARDENER

I can see him now,
Hands on hips,
Planning the sequence
Of his small rotation.
Can see the rows
Of brassicas and beans -
The rakes and hoes
Leaning at angles
On the garden shed.
A rose reflects
The roundness of his face -
Seems somehow strained
And reddened by exertion.
The ground remains
As stubborn as it was -
Prefers the weed
To vegetables and flowers.
Impervious to winter rain
An inch of tilth
Drains its consistence
To the dregs of slurry.
In summer heat - resistant
To the sharpest spade -
The clay cracks chasms
On the edge of harvest.
I can see him now,
Day after fruitless day,
Wielding defiance
Like a heavy mattock -
Can see his back
Bent bare against
Diagonals of light,
Bronze - like a statue -
And as uncomplaining.

DERIVATIVE (BEELEIGH ESSEX)

Confluence and outlet:
Two rivers, two locks,
Two weirs and a waterfall.
A creek that veers
Dependant on the tides
And a slow canal
Choked to the gunwales
With a green persistence.
Revolve and see
The centuries that turn:
Buildings that were
  now ghosted
Into copse and thicket -
Timber and stone
Settled to the sediments
  of time
And the once great elms
Broken to splinters
By the rack of fungus.
Think how the landscape
  alters:
How the banks and ditches
Channel the waters
Of our slow achievement -
While the silts between
  them
Build to the bridges
Of ingrown succession.
Somewhere the thunder
  booms:
A swallow swerves to
Figuring's of eight
And blooms on a far
  green bush
Burst from an island
Like a pink enigma.

JANUARY DUSK

The blackbird chinks
Its stridency of notes -
Sharp and yet hollow
Like the ring of ice.

The wind speaks harshly
Of the frozen north
  and clothes
On the swaying line
Stiffen to cut-outs
On a screen of stratus.

Water in a white dish
Bends its meniscus
To a cold translucence
And the snow-sunk garden
Clings under hedges
To its quilt of leaves.

SEPTEMBER MORNING

The sun's an infusion through the morning mist -
A golden draught of summer's breath distilled
Slowly fermenting on the scent of autumn.

The brambles twist their labyrinths of thorn -
Out-spin on air such silences of silk
To catch the wings of cold-condensing light.

ARGUMENT IN AUTUMN

How the thought of loss affects me -
The leaves apportion blame, promises so nearly kept
Shedding their statements on a swoon of colour.

Your voice, nothing but an echo -
A ghost, that once, consoling and assured
Can now express but solitude and sadness.

Your image now, impossible to frame:
As vague as seems this cold October sky -
Silent and sombre with its share of secrets.

When will I change the meanings -
Replace the loss with warm configurations?

Find words again in everything I see:
Where nothing moves unconscious of your form -
Holds and caresses, like a known sensation?

PLAYGROUND

I remember your expression:
The way you smiled after conquest -
Was it the winning that made you so,
Or that grin the deflection of a growing guilt?

You knew that I was easily beaten -
    No kudos to be gained.

I lay on the ground pretending to be hurt -
    All was intact; except my pride.

I thought that my defeat would be enough:
That you would be contented with applause -

But no, you'd tasted blood:
Has cause to make your victory complete -
One final kick, one foul, yet human gesture.

SUMMER STORM

The valley shudders
Like a muffled drum -
Deep in the compass
Of the air's percussion.

The rain to come
Limits the vision
To dissolving hills
And the first, few drops,
Burst into movement
Through sporadic leaves.

A singing chaffinch
Rattles to a sudden stop
And a far, soft cadence
Drifts from the willows
Like a drowning echo.

This, the interregnum:
The sun deposed
Hides its dejection
Under robes of cloud -

Hemlock and hogweed
Skulk in the shadows
Like unnerved retainers
And the grass bows meekly
To the wind's dictation.

FLY

Despised by most -
Not seen beyond
Its deathly connotations.

Progenitor of that which crawls
And sucks the juice
Of all that deliquesces.

Yet look again -
See eyes that breast
Their facets to the sun
And cleave the light
To cuts of iridescence.

See wings like leaves
Un-fleshed into the veins
That swim on air
Their filamentous film
And blur the mind
To single-frame impressions.

Hear sound disclaim
All reference to size
Where life as loud
As issues from the child
Adds its vibration
To the list of being.

A RICH PRESERVE

All can remember blackberrying:
Each their own lane or riverside walk -
An alley through a dark copse,
Or the field's blue edge
Shaded to corners under clumps of elm.
All have encountered the richest smells:
The sweet-dank tips of the fingers,
    Prickled and purple -
Remember the leaves in red-green whorls
Fading to yellow at the hint of autumn.
Nothing quite as succulently tells
Of summers past or winters yet to come:
    The last slow heat -
    The dying wasp -
    The fly's deep drone
Dreaming and drowsing through its glint
    Metallics.
All have the oozings of their own nostalgia -
    Their own brim jars
Crammed and compacted with the fruits
    Of distance.

RIVER ALBUM

We know this place -
Have made it something special.

We trace the seasons through the camera's eye -
Make images mechanical with light
To frame our thoughts like memories in aspic.

Just you and I and the river's cold transparency:
The negatives of ever changing sky
Sliding beneath us on the edge of focus -

The deep-deceptive spirit of our lives
Doubled and distant - like a slow exposure.

CAPTAIN

Never saw a ship, but liked the uniform -
Swung on his gate, white hat and gold braid,
For all the world a salt retired,

"Morning mates!
Good weather for a trip,
Wind's in the right quarter."

We never thought it strange,
Eccentric perhaps, but harmless -
His house, a craft of sorts,
Chimneys under full smoke,
An orchard, thick with masts and yards.

I've seen him list through a tide of cabbages -
Rolling to landward under swigs of rum.

"Drop a grog me hearties,
Come aboard,
I'll spin yer a yarn."

We never went, lubbers to a man -
The last I remember was a wreck of limbs,
Sprawled by the windfalls, in a sea of bottles.

ON THE VERGE

This lane our loving tunnel:
Our autumn game of kiss and consummation -
Drawing us under into spells of colour.

How well we know its ways - its climb and curve -
Its slow caressing compass of the fields
Merging with shadows like an assignation.

Each twist reveals some unexpected facet:
A limb of light shedding its raiment
    Through the furtive branches.

    Berries as voluptuous as lips,
Full red and rounded on the verge of passion:
The sloes, like eyes enhanced through belladonna -
Gleaming and glancing with their blue-black secrets.

1986 - 1990

MIDNIGHT

So cold, so calm:
The grass crackles underfoot -
Reflects the moon
From cuts of many angles.

Diamond or paste -
Glass or crystal?

So clear, so cruel:
So bitter yet so beautiful
  this ice -
That like a fool
I stand beneath the stars
And sacrifice my sentience to zero.

A SILENT UNDERSTANDING

Before the words, we knew what would be said -
Each other's mind, so seeming unconcerned,
Had read the thought that spun its line between us.

These threads we knew as something never learnt –
Like silks that shine in complicated webs
To redefine the simplest of vibrations.

TO STAUNCH A WOUND

She pinned a spray of tansies to her blouse:
Held out her hand for me to catch the smell -
To understand the sharp September fragrance.

I know too well the tang that autumn brings -
Remember, once, that I could not foretell
The things we love would heal our separation.

HIC TRANSIT GLORIA MUNDI

Have you ever been to church on Christmas Eve,
When people lurching homeward from the pub
Hear 'Silent Night' sung loudly, and believe -
Are taken back to innocent perceptions?

They enter in and weave between the pews:
This once a year, when they, no longer lost -
No more confused by trifling resentments
Rejoin the flock and celebrate the shepherd.

The frankincense effuses in a cloud,
So pungent, so impossible to breathe,
That in a blur they slump amid the sounds
Of organ keys and adolescent voices.

The chancel spins - a whir of votive candles -
The tableau and the lights upon the tree
Merge each with each their colours as they swim
And angel's wings seem more than mere rehearsals.

They focus for an instant in the dark
As one gold star falls earthwards from the beams -
Sing 'Gloria - in slurred - Excelsis Deo'
And then they sleep, through snores of adoration.

CLIFFTOWN

A Wednesday afternoon, the summer in retreat
And autumn's tune, not rousing, like a march
But beat by beat through colours of detachment.

The quiet streets are cast in such a light
That scours stone and bleaches stubborn brick;
Until, though each, so different to the eye,
Become as one in subtleties of yellow.

The bowling-green is peopled yet apart -
Composed as if a score upon a sheet,
Where shadows mark the tempo of the leaves
That drop their notes, like brass, diminuendo.

BILLINGSGATE

In Thames Street, once, the lower end I think,
Where barrows wheeled on heavy iron rims
Go clank and clink on early morning cobbles;
I saw a man manoeuvring a fish -
A fish so big that one could only blink
To see its nose so distant from its tail.

Another there, with baskets on his head:
Stacked seven high with halibut and eels -
Would snake and slink with cheeks so round and red
'less he should spill his undulating cargo.

And then, now you must take this with a wink,
Believe me or deny me at your will -
Great squares of ice, like glass without the chink,
Were cut and thrown with such transparent skill,
That where they fell and slid across the brink
The darkest door was luminous with sparkles.

SPRING FLOWER

The sepals open
Like an envelope to steam.

    Inside,
    The longed-for secrets:

The perfumed paper -
Heady with the scent
        of assignations.

    A stigma,
    With a style of its own:

Anthers
    in the bee's
        unsteady hand -

The pollen grains
For future correspondence.

BLACKBIRD

Mellifluous songster -
Black as beginnings
On the edge of spring.
Composer with a gold nib -
Crotchet and quaver
Of the dawn's notation.
Pan-piper -
Flute-feather -
Wind in the weather
Of the woken woods
Singing of sorrel
And the stars of stitchwort.
Leaf-raker -
Worm-snatcher -
Chider of cruel cats
Coiled like serpents
In a cleft of sunlight.
Ditch-delver -
Lawn-hopper -
Rhyme to remember
In a court of kings -
Brim to the coffers
With a song that silvers.

TRACKS

So quiet, only the woods and snow -
A few haphazard tracks,
Enough it seems to emphasise the silence.

Step on a twig:
Listen to the snap that volleys -
That ricochets forever into distance.

The fields beyond,
Like vast unwritten pages -
Nothing grows, nothing happens.

A pheasant strolls,
Like words between the covers -
Opens a chapter of exotic language.

ELIM LIL

ELIM Lil, evangelist in a tin shack -
        Poor Clare to rats and magpies.
Said prayers aloud -
   sang hymns beneath ecclesiastic branches.
A paradise to her:
     bullace and greengage,
         bread for the small birds,
             plums for an autumn Eucharist.
The children used to watch her
                    at the well -
Rebbeca in a shift of rags.
Perhaps there was some latter day
                  St Francis -
Some loss of love remembered and revered
That turned her heart
         from earth's dissatisfactions.
Selfless yet sufficient:
Vegetables and cottage flowers,
Timber, cut and stacked against the frost.
On winter nights the sacrament of candles -
The votive glare from windows otherworldly.

GRANDMOTHER

My grandmother was like a kangaroo -
Not that she was Australian, or used to hop about;
Like most octogenarians she was better
                            at the shuffle than the leap.
In fact, she was part Irish -
Something in common with most grandmothers.
No, it was that apron, that inviting pouch,
Marsupial with pegs and Woodbines.
Such was the fascination to a child -
The lucky dip:
Hairpins and bits of string,
A bottle-opener for her Guinness.
There were things in there deeper than Australia -
Higher than the stars at Christmas:
A handkerchief with twisted corners -
One lick and eyes were cleared of blots and irritations;
Plasters and boiled sweets -
Sticky with their different reasons.
She could conjure anything:
Pennies from her purse -
Words as rich and wild as 'shenanigan'.
    "Mighty fine,"
        she used to say,
           "mighty fine."
I don't know what it means, but I know she meant it.
Half leprechaun, half saint,
She tyrannised with smiles and invective.
Crippled with sciatica and love
She managed life a mix of ice and fire -
As volatile and silent as a storm
She passed away and filled the world with shadows.

BIRD-NESTING

I recall a blackbird's nest, hidden in brambles -
A woven cup of mud and grass,
Protected by the whiplash briars.

How great the temptation -
Four smooth eggs,
Blue-green and mottled brown.

I didn't mind the scratches -
The beads of blood
    smeared to a trickle
        down the arms and legs.

It was a clutch of treasure -a test -
Something to be proud of.

I used a thorn to pierce the shell - then blew -
Nothing came,
    no pallid yolk,
        no thick translucence.

The air around rattled with the parents' chiding:
The shell peeled whitely to the foetal flesh -
To the small pink bud - barely pulsating.

AMAZONIAN CLONE PARABLE

Adam and Evil were naked,
"an apple a day," said the snake,
with a sort of Hippocratic malevolence.

Evil said, "I'd sooner be beauty,"
so Adam bit her ear
and she became deaf to the core.

Adam, found his looks adorable -
couldn't give a fig for God
and saw himself the object of reflection.

Evil said, that Adam was a madam -
Adam, fell madly in love
with the suggestion, and drowned.

Evil, by herself, was sorry for ribbing Adam
and made amends by wearing a robe
and becoming immaculate.

When she gave birth to her own father's son,
        she was confused -
could not conceive of parthenogenesis.

The doctor blamed the symptoms on neurosis:
she knew a snake-in-the-grass, when she saw one -
she sloughed her skin; turned ugly, with genetics.

BEANFLOWERS

Autumn impinges, even though it's spring:
       just a word, 'beanflowers.'

"Too late last year," she said,
"Too late to come to anything."

How does a word hold so much power?
No need to close my eyes, to concentrate;
The scarlet blooms, just grow there, like a vision.

I can feel the heat, the calm, October weather:
Chrysanthemums and dahlias, bleaching in sunlight - smoke,
       like a blue ghost,
Climbing the trellis into air unfathomed.

       What now?
The daffodils have tarnished in the shadows -
       turned to rust.
Tulips, like closed fists,
Suffer with their swollen veins -
              ease into redness.

She leaves her seat to walk across the lawn -
       tugs at a few weeds.
The early bees are cumbersome with sound -
          a swallow, cuts a corner, clings, like ice.

A QUESTION OF BRIDGES

What is it about bridges -
Not just the way
              they look,
The rhythms of their piers
   and arches;
Nor yet the fascination
          of the stream,
Splayed by the buttress
       into light divided.
Even the tree that falls -
That lodges bank to bank
And agitates
      the fluency of water.
Even this, like stones
That cross,
      haphazardly inclined,
To guide the feet
     through fathomless
          transactions.
What is it that we seek -
   the other side,
The joining
 of incomparable halves,
Or just the span
To test an act of balance?

WEIRPOOL

The wind through aspens
Echoes the river
    as it leaps the weir.
A wagtail's yellow
              flicker,
Doubles with sunlight
Through the plumes
        of spray -
Worries the spectrum
    into shifts of focus.
Nettles and cleavers
Sharpen their incense
    on the edge of silt -
Spatter the clothing
With their green stigmata.
A chub,
       noses into light -
Then buries
       its own gold.
Irreligious coots
Shatter the icons
    of intense reflection -
Bicker like skeptics
    in a shrine of rushes.

WATERCOLOUR

By an island in the Crouch -
Where the widgeon whistle
And the slow, slouch tide
Catches the fire
Of the falling sunlight -
Where the windows
In a wooden shack
Blaze to the blueness
Of a frosted sky
And their tide-wrack embers
Delve into doubles
On the dowse of river.

By an island in the Crouch -
Where the buoys bob yellow
Through the brine of dusk
And the sea-silk oils
Slide through the shallows
Into silts and saltings -
Where the wide, wet marshes
Cast their reflections
In a web of water
And the far, flute curlew
Curve like a calmness
To the moon's momentum.

SPELL

That evening in June, when we walked the river;
    the moon exactly halved -
A ghost at the zenith, while the sun still lingered.

We two, amongst the comfrey and the mallow,
Talking in whispers, like the trees above us.

Was it the fishermen who encouraged us to silence?
Or the thought that something other -
Some startled bird or levitating fish
Might break the spell and shatter our reflections?

I only know, that fallow field was best -
The mayweed and the poppies unresolved,
Their colours blent of innocence and passion.

To see you there, through shadows dressed with gold,
Diffuse, as if evolving from a dream;
Was something told, that I cannot forget -
Will yet redeem when light has lost its swallows.

TIMEPIECE

I see them all:
I watch them through
The turning of my hands -
The young, the old,
The slow, the quick.

They do not surprise me -
Each one in time
Will lift me from the shelf
And turn the key
That activates my being.

I feel inside
The tick of my existence -
The cogs and cams,
The wheels and balances.

Beside me are the
Photographs in frames -
The this and that
Of passing generations.

My pendulum enumerates
The silence -
Counts out the days
And punctuates the darkness.

I see them all:
Their transient desires -
The full, the fit,
The empty and the tired.

I feel the tension
Easing from my springs -
The sense of loss
That spirals from my face.

The room expands
Beyond the reach of hours -
In every eye
The helix of division.

CLOSING THE TILL

"Come along gents,
You're well past time."

How the words cut in -
Truth is, it's time
That's passing us.

How many glasses drained -
    how many nights
Of cigarettes and laughter?

The same faces -
The same conversations:
Prices and politics,
Marriage and divorce,
Cars and unemployment.

The barmaid wriggles
    to the till,
And eyes, like sharks,
Swim to the rhythms
Of her buoyant flesh.

She darts a glance
That shimmers in the smoke -
Rings up 'no sale',
Then slams the message home.

KINGFISHER

It moves so fast
It's gone before it's seen -

A was it there, unconscious,
Conscious thing, that cuts the air
And splays the eye with colour.

An orange flame:
A blue ignition -

A word above the water where it stops
To over-stare its own exalted image.

A famous name that dares to drop itself -
That there enfolds the flicker of its fire
And shatters the humility of minnows.

SAILING BARGES

The barges line the quay. By twos
Abreast they settle on the ooze
And wait the tides to lift their keels
To seaward. Across the saltings
The trees remember trade, how things
Were once, before the open fields.

Long gone the adze, the many skills
Of men, who knew the grain that yields
Against the storm. A few remain,
Enthusiasts or aged salts.
Those men who find the modern course
Too much, and drag corroded chains.

LACHRYMA CHRISTI

There's a hole in the sky -
It's true; I've seen it.

It must be a hole
Because things fall through.

Once, the rain attacked me -
Bruised me with its cold voice.

I shut my eyes:
Pretended that I couldn't hear -

Felt dry tears sharpen their edges
On the air's thin membrane.

In spring, swallows and cuckoos
Tumble with sunshine
Through a chute of shadows -
    It's true,
The trees are full of them.

Nothing can escape -
Perhaps a rocket or an angel.

But then, what's up there -
A string of pearls,
A million gems,
Snow by the shovel-full.

Best if they close it up for good -
Fill it with rainbows
And a goose for Christmas.

EASTERLY

Snow in April -
Like mimic blossom
Falling obliquely
To confuse the earth.

The winter wheat:
Twelve inches into summer -
Reaching through whispers
For the wings of swallows.

The season of rebirth:
Swaddled in white,
Edged in gold -
Some how at odds
And yet appropriate.

The robin, its own parody -
An image of an earlier event
Framed by the matrix
Of reluctant flowers.

NIGHT WATCH

The hour after midnight -
The streets un-peopled and the floral gardens
Loud in the silence of unopened petals.

The estuary, strewn with light -
With the port and starboard of uncertain journeys.

A siren sounds its solitary note -
Harsh, yet inviting, through a bloom of mist.

The stars astound, like asphodels on fire -
Delve through the darkness
To the roots of vision.

DEMYSTIFIED

If you could see the jay -
Could take your eyes' incision to its wing
And cut away the carapace of colour.

Could part the smooth histology of skin
And count beneath the calculus of bone -

Could further cut, as curious as knives,
That sever there the sinews of belief
And find the heart a burden in its cage.

What else but grief would suffer your surprise -
Would freeze the cold-coagulate of thought
And leave the air as sentient as death?

MEHALAH'S ISLE

(for the Rev. Sabine Baring Gould who was rector of East
Mersea in Essex and wrote the book: Mehalah - a story of the
salt-marsh)

The drama still pervades -
Sharp as the salt-sea wind
The written words
Still build there waves to landward.

Mehalah's land,
Out paragraphed by time -
Still haunts the strood
And whispers through the marsh.

From Salcott church the sun suffusing red
Reminds me yet of Rebow's blinding anger.

On creek and cove
The passing light inclines -
Rewrites the florid passage of the dead
And leaves the tide its last reflective chapter.

The fictive air resolves the cleric's thoughts -
Reveals the cold denouement of a ghost.

PLOTLANDS

Marginal they said -
The clay, fretted with fissures
And the August sun
Draining the ditches
Through its straws of grass.

A land of scrub and thicket -
Of unnumbered bees
Humming and heavy
With the weight of pollen.

A place of unceasing sound -
The rasp and rattle
Of the crickets' music;

And the distant quaver
Of a lark-lost ripple
Rising and falling
Like a flute through water.

Marginal they said -
Thistles with purple plumes
Spilling their fire
On the wings of burnets.

All heat and haze -
Buttercups and poppies
Drawn by the breezes
To a forge of colour.

The yellowhammer's
Utterance of air -
Whistled and wheezy
Like the breath of bellows.

RESURRECTION

It scratches from beneath -
Claws at the soil
Through a night of shivers.

The corpse must have release -
Must lift the lid
Of slow increasing light
And breathe again
The gift of warming air.

Its fingers show
With tips of green -
Such slender hands
To shift the frozen earth.

The trees imbibe its blood -
Prepare through buds
To bourgeon into leaf
And ring their girth
On corpuscles of gold.

Tissue by tissue
Its body builds -
Hedge and copse
Flesh out their bones
And the fields unwrinkle
Into crops and flowers.

The long-entombed
Leaves winter in its stead -
Strides through the woodland
With the voice of angels.

COMPULSORY PURCHASE (Basildon New Town)

We grew our gardens
From the tilth of others -
Those plotland few
Evicted by our needs.

The barrow-loads of soil,
Whole trees and cuttings,
Glass and timber -
They all received
Our flowering attention.

But now it seems
The victory short-lived -
Pyrrhic only.

The town unfurls
And light reflects
A double-glazed stomata.

The pulsing streets
Are vascular with noise -
That gooseberry bush
A green memento-mori.

HOLY WEEK

When April comes
And winter's breath
No longer haunts the air;

When early sun comes
Blazing from the depths
And dares the eye
To dazzle with the dawn;

Like one whose slept
Through cold-unnumbered years
To find the breach
Where sentience is born
And touch the pulse
Of all created being;

When darkness dies
And all the west
Unwritten by its stars
Defines the edge
Of luminous horizons;

When flowers test
The sanctity of light
To bloom and bless
The season of the heart;

Then what is left
To limit the surprise -
Save those two arms
And Christ's inclining head.

FEBRUARY

A month between seasons -
Gold in one hand, ice in the other.

The doves invest in syllables of light
Despite the rain that delves a fallen index.

One might suppose with 'fill-dyke' as a name
That nothing flows but brown and viscous water.

Be not deceived:

If snow or drench or anything of power
Believes itself more artful than the spring -

Then watch the seed that hunches in the earth
To make its bid and clinch the air with flowers.

WHITE LIGHT

I'm still unsure of Sundays -
Their slow pace, sad
With the sermon of remembered echoes.

I never see a chapel or a church
Without my mind unlatching at the door
To search along the rows of retrospection.

I know that I will never find the past
Between the stone that arches, and the aisle;

But sometimes when the memory is cast
Like light that splays from windows to the floor,
I see again the image of the saints
As something more than icons of the spectrum.

AUGUST BANK HOLIDAY

The mudflats are
Green with zostera.

Gullies and standing water
Combine with sky
Through blue and liquid silver.

Masts lean at haphazard angles
And gulls' wings
Curve against harsh sounds.

People on the gravel hard
Walk towards sandbanks
And the distant sea -

Sink into shimmers
Through the haze of August.

Summer is a blown glass -
Molten and edgeless
In the breath of sunlight.

A SAD EXPRESSION

I am aware of walking in this place:
Of something that I call the sun -
Of sky and clouds and attitudes of space
That air describes as movement through the leaves.
I see, or so my senses seem to trace,
    a distant line of hills -
Some colours, or the different length of waves
That sink and spill from object and illusion.

But more than these, or platitudes of grace
That time distils to save me from myself,
I see again the sadness in your face -
The sadness that humanity reveals
When nature neither watches nor relates
But hides beneath the countenance of shadows.

CUCKOO LAND

We do not own it, but it's ours:
The subtle changes are our property -

The endless transformations of the clouds
Filling the coffers of a stateless summer.

The birds have territory to defend -
Parameters of song.

We turn our pockets out:
Ignore the fences -
Belong to no-one but ourselves.

We feed on love, like bees
That drown in pollen.

Yet still I doubt the coinage of the flowers:
My spendthrift words -
The tongue's unsound collateral.

AGNOSTIC

He was always drawn to churches -
Their timeless architecture.

He didn't believe in God -
At least not God as written in the Bible.

He remembered the rites, the solemn rituals -
Found genuflection easy if alone
And came to prayer as simple as a child.

He knelt before the cross and closed his eyes
To feel again the sacrament of silence.

Could sense once more the pulse of other lives -
The resonance of hope and aspiration
That time accrues in sanctuaries of stone.

APRIL THE FIRST

        The light dissembles after rain -
   curves to the colours
Of untold deflections.

The leaves cast early shadows:
     their green surmisals -
          bold against the stark anatomies.

Narcissi, wallow in their own illusions -
Each cold, white echo,
     mouthing its zero in a star's circumference.

   The sun is evanescent:
Its gift of gold, a hoax amongst the clouds -
Caught, like the swallow that purports a summer.

THE ESOTERIC ANGLER

He knew the river well -
Was fluent with its meanings.

Though asked to tell
His answers were evasive -
Kept to the margins,
Like a shoal of secrets.

Equivocation was his lure -
Meanderings his disposition.

No one for sure could
Penetrate the depths -
Fathom the contents
In his mesh of words.

Once hooked and held secure,
He waited till you leapt
Towards the light;

Then slowly with
A deftness that procures,
He drew you in
And ministered the priest.

(Priest - blunt instrument for dispatching fish)

THE TREATMENT

I worked on a sewage-farm once:
The only place that it didn't smell
    was in the toilet -
That's where I used to eat my lunch.

Outside, where the sediments had settled -
Where the rank excreta
Was cut and stacked to dry beneath the sun;
Tomato plants hung heavy with their fruits.

    Despite the flies,
The older men still picked them -
Still took them home to supplement their wages.

The only thing I left with was the stench:
Enough to be the butt of all my friends -
Their noses pinched; their bum-fluff innuendo.

HEDGEHOG PIE

The gypsies still had wagons in the fifties,
Their tethered horses browsing by the verge;

I never saw a hedgehog cooked or eaten
But still believed the myth was more than words.

I used to watch them quietly through the hawthorn,
Their kettles black and steaming on the fire,

"Who'll buy my lucky lavender," she whispered,
Her eyes so dark they startled with desire;

And as I ran, her laughter ran beside me,
Her voice as bold and blatant as her dress,

"Be lucky boy, be careful of the gypsies,"
And as I turned my mind, was no, and yes.

NEW TOWN

How the town was then
in its slow sleep
never again
to be found un-growing
in the sky-wet
weep of the leaves
over slippery paths
where the sly smell
reeks and remembers
of a fox-brown autumn
there where the rank air
turns on its tendrils
to a twine of ivy
and the blue-black
sloes in the hedgerows
bend over brambles
on a bloom of berries
never again
in the sun-slick
sheen over water
and the wisp of willows
where the branch-bare
rooks in a revel
pepper with purple
the surrounding elms
what of the witch
and the one-eyed man
in the ditch-dark
path by the windows
of their lamp-lit hovels
where the moon's arc
climbs from the copses
on the lips of owls
and the bat's wing
sweeps like a besom
through a blink of shadows
there in the star-still
step of Orion
over half the sky
as the light's chill
cools and condenses

to the wink of frost
there in the lost land
in the long past moss
and the mildew
of another ruin
in the snow-soft rut-hard
white of a winter
that has gone forever
what of the spring
and the waiting sisters
of the goose-grey
cold into April
and the clutch of Easter
of their old age
shell-thin
frail in the fortune
of an ancient holding
what of the sun
and the scent of summer
of the dog-rose
dog-star
death and denial
of their golden harvest.

WALKING GANGER

Sack'em Joe we call him -
Lackey to the foreman and the agent.
He knows his place, and ours -
Arranges life round starting-times and tea-breaks.

One of the half-hunter brigade:
Gold chain and waistcoat -
Cloth cap and corduroys.

He's always there when he isn't wanted:
Stop for a chat and up he pops,
Scowling down his long nose -
Goading the rabbits with his weasel features.

I suppose he enjoys it:
The hypnotic stare -
His status as protected species.

Sometimes we answer back:
Dare him as he reddens and reviles -
Spits out the venom that his wage determines.

Today, in a meadow thick with flowers,
He strings a line for over-site and footings.
We watch him as he circles and assesses -
Measures the moment for his next attack.

He stands there as we dig and bottom-out -
Unnerves us, as we sweat within the warren.

CULTIVATION

Although these cauliflowers
Have all the appearance
Of being brains,
It is a well known fact
That earlier in their evolution
They were nothing more than cabbages.

What this means for the roses
Growing in amongst them
I wouldn't like to say,
Except, perhaps, in passing
That despite the thorns and the manure
Roses, have got to grow, somewhere.

LANDING

Walk out again:
Look at the marshes -
The sweep of the seawall.

Imagine what it was like
To live there, or there,
Different time, different weather.

The rooks create a marquetry:
Black against blue ground -
Movement in the year's first stillness.

You can smell the heat -
Feel it, like a memory.

A barge lies broken on the mud -
Ribs and vertebra, shattered, prehistoric.

Crabs move sideways -
Scuttle in irons.

A shelduck curves to laughter up the reach -
Spreads out its wings; cuts swarf from water.

TWITCHER

I sit here listening to the birds:
Before the migrants come -
Before their words are lost to other voices.

It's what they tell you in the books -
The way to learn, to separate.

Listen, there's a wren, loud for its size:
Consider the final trill -
That rattle, like a signature, a coda.

There's the dunnock, shrill and scratchy -
Dapper in its own way, a touch colonial,
Needs a veranda, a punka-wallah.

Is that a robin? Yes - it must be,
Nothing else as purposeful, pugnacious;
But wistful too, listen it decants another note -
The setting sun, like burgundy, like claret.

HEAVENWARDS

There's not much grace
when a swan takes wing -
what with weight
and gravity in opposition
and the skin of water
losing its tension
to the webbed assault;

it's hard to think
of anything like finesse
when every thought
has laughter as its link
to test the bonds
of beauty and deportment;

but when it springs
long-headed into flight,
beyond the walk
absurdly over waves
it brings to earth
an aspect of delight
that names itself
the element of angels.

STANLEY ROAD

It wasn't paradise
nothing to do with innocence
goats and a few chickens
a plot for vegetables.

They managed somehow
mother and daughter
both pensioners.

No country idyll though
pebble-dash and tin
poor substitute for thatch.

An Elsan by the hedge
a stagnant pond
rabbits in a hutch.

I don't remember
when they left, or died?
it didn't matter much
not to a child.

I found a magic lantern
in the loft
some coloured slides
some candles.

We knocked the veranda down
smashed windows
raided the orchard.

It always smelt of autumn
leaves in the ditch
fermenting fruit.

I'll never forget
that elderberry wine
the tainted lips
the body's retribution.

HANDING IN THE KEYS

Never again will I see that garden
the doors are closed
the keys relinquished.

The past is where it always was
secure in the mind
part of the memory.

Her ghost will always haunt it though
"You can't beat Coxes;
I like the taste of my own potatoes."

Secateurs in hand
ready to prune
on the lookout for cuttings.

Last year she layered strawberries
planted a few bulbs.

Who knows what gold the spring may yet assume -
what summers grow to tempt another's lips?

I only know the severing of roots
the stench of earth
the urgency of sunlight.

PARKS AND GARDENS

More parks and gardens, that's what we need:
Somewhere to sit and doze beneath the trees
Or to watch the seasons that are young forever.

Somewhere to age more gracefully,
Like potted plants in rows beneath the sun
To catch the heat or soften under showers.

We need to be treated with more respect,
Like flowers in the Corporation beds,
Nurtured and worthy of the hoe's attention.

We too were heeled-in once, breathers of the same air:
Why do you see us as if now estranged -
Weeds in the garden that was once our Eden?

You too may come to wear an autumn face -
Be rooted to this bench beneath the trees
As leaf on leaf disseminates, like sadness.

ROBIN

I cannot see the singer
    but the song
Holds autumn in the sadness of its scale,
Like leaves that fall to realise their shadows
When gold no longer lingers nor prevails.

The sun's as pale as pebbles
    or a primrose
That finds itself a refugee from spring,
I cannot see the solitary singer
But every note has winter on its wing.

I cannot hold the summer
    but its ghost
Lies golden with the lichen on the wall,
The song's as thin as something nearly over
And down the air the music floats and falls.

BIRD-WATCHING

I watched a warbler hawking butterflies -
Hovering like a kestrel by the loosestrife.

A cuckoo, several times the warbler's size,
Waited with a wide gape
For fresh supplies of cabbage-whites and commas.

Next year, when spring, with double-note surprise
Awakens thoughts of summer fields and flowers,
I'll think again how beauty paid the price -
How paradise was fed on angel's wings.

TESTING THE WATER

The day, so warm, so welcome .
"A walk in the stream, barefoot?
You'll never do it," she said,
"You're too old, you don't mean it."

The challenge was too great -
A simple thing, a gesture.

    How cold it was -
How deep with her beside me was the ache,
As if my bones had something to remember.

MAY THE FIFTH

The arrival of the swifts -
For days I've watched,
   nothing;
And yet here they are,
Five on the evening air
Curved into substance
By the thought of summer.

Cuneiform on blue papyrus -
Fluent with contrast;
All night they'll fly -
Ink to the sky's ink,
Lost to the liquid
Of the leaching stars.

   Tomorrow,
When the flowers wake -
When the words of fragrance
Climb on the voices
Of the warming earth;
They'll underline
The languages they make -
Screech over paper,
Like a nib that scratches.

SUMMER NIGHT

One of those summer nights, one of the few -
When sound alights and calls itself a thrush
From some tall tree, half shadow and half fire.

One when the swifts are rushing into blue -
Are tag and touch, like children of the sky,
Whose only care is catch me if you can.

One when the air so heavy with its hush
Reads out the banns of marriage to the moon -
When scented stocks, delirious at dusk,
Invite the moths to dance amongst their flowers.

WATCHING SWALLOWS

Leaning across the bridge's parapet,
Looking down, at two who are looking up,
We watch the swallows flying there between us.

We listen for the sound of wings,
But cannot hear them:
They glide as if the air is oiled -
As if the wind has lost the willow's voice.

We notice how their backs are sheened with blueness:
How poised they are when hawking for a fly -
And having seen, we drop a few remarks,
That echo through the arches underneath us.

CATERPILLARS

I feel cocooned within this wood,
As if enmeshed by gossamers that spin
And ferry gold from sunlight through the leaves.

    Is this where I begin -
A second womb transforming by belief,
Dissolving flesh, and challenging ideas?

And when, like these that loop along my arm
Will I exchange my heaviness for wings -
Or like that snail, grow cumbersome with horns?

ON-LINE

They've taken the trees down by the railway track -
Painted the station red and blue and gold.

They said they needed a new image -
That the old ways wouldn't do.

Who knows? Perhaps they're right,
Anyway who needs the sky's mosaic -
The song of birds to serenade their sunsets?

The tannoy teaches all we need to know -
How late the train is; the garbled destinations.

FEBRUARY THE TWENTY-NINTH

Only yesterday she said it -
"Look here!" she said,
"You do the washing, and
The cooking, and
The sowing, and
I'll get on with the bloody garden
And worry about being the bread winner.

Well, I just don't know what gets into her -
What it is she gets so upset about.

I took me feet down off the mantle-shelf,
Tipped me pipe out in the fireplace,
Stood up, and prepared to give her
The regulation bollocking.

"Look," I said, thumbs behind braces,
    Chest prominent,
"It's about time we got something straight."

It was about then
That I felt the pain in my testicles.
I like a woman with a bit of spunk,
Y'know, but then, there are limits, surely.

"Christ!" I excruciated, "what the friggin'
    Hell d'you do that for?"

Without another word
She brought her knee up under my chin,
Grabbed me firmly by the ears
And started knocking me 'ead against the wall.

"Mind the ducks, darling," I said,
"Mother bought those for our wedding."

    "Fuck the ducks!"
Was her less than polite response.
"As far as I'm concerned,
You can stuff 'em right up your rectory."

Well, I thought,
Lovely sentiment from a vicar's daughter.
One wonders where all this liberation's
   Leading to.

RITUALISTIC

The places that attract us year by year
To carry out our ritual enactments.

The hedgerows that were suddenly severe
When winter dawn with ice had made its pact

And thorns were clear, uncannily with crystal;
Are now as near to paradise on earth

With sun and silk colluding through the mist
To catch the fruits of summer's mere rehearsals.

The sloe, as if a pupil that dilates,
With blear and bloom in soft, September skies,

Is sweet, then dry, then sour to the taste
Of any tongue that memory surprises.

The bramble with its dank, delicious drupes,
Still tempts the hand, despite the droning wasp

Who guards the rank and rasping convolutions.
No season holds the sentiment of loss

With such a spell that aggregates to gold
And fills the mind with ripening delusions.

The mushrooms lie, like relics in the cold,
And dusk reveres the sacrament of frost.

JOURNEYS

When I travel:
Make contact with the astral -
Speak tongues to elementals;
I feel at home.

It's this side seems the journey -
Gravity, time and space,
Ungainly movement.

There it's different:
The soul unravels
From its crude complexities -
Reforms, like crystal.

I do not envy the unborn:
The soluble in darkness -
Their turn's to come;
Their once in a lifetime,
Or twice, or thrice,
Or any nightmare
That the gods determine.

Now that the journey's over:
The sun seems powerless -
In fact does not exist.

What light there is
Is neither hot nor cold -
As for the stars, they cut no ice.

MIDDLE-AGE

I borrowed me brother's double-breasted,
Just the number for the weekly dance.
Whether it went with the hound's-tooth check,
The winkle pickers, I wouldn't like to say.
I felt good though, in with a chance,
    Know what I mean?

Sixteen, hair slicked back, Tony Curtis,
Duck's arse, fag at a leery angle.
I wasn't much of a dancer, held back,
You know, waited for the slow ones.
I can't remember her name, Maisie or Pat,
    I'm not sure now.

You know the type though, hooped-skirt,
Masses of petticoats, stockings and suspenders.
Funny, it didn't seem erotic then,
Lust was purer in those days.
Anyway, enough of that old nonsense,
    On with the story.

WATER-SPLASH

Always the water-splash -
Time and again
We find ourselves beside it.

It is our natural place -
A magnet to our
Un-deciphered being.

The arching trees
Are vaulted, like a brain -
A cortex made from
Interlocking branches.

No-one explains it -
This head we live in.

The sunlight strikes
The quick synaptic leaves
And shadows drain
Subjectively to earth.

The water swirls away -
Distorts the real
With images of chaos.

We lift our eyes
And light is rearranged -
More positive, though
Haunted with reflections

YOUNG BARN-OWLS

Monsters, feathered gargoyles,
Eyes as black as beetles,
Legs, like wire, twisted into talons.

He feeds them chicks,
Soft, yellow down,
And pink, near putrid flesh.

They gulp and gorge, grotesquely,
Digest the indigestible.

Four freaks that death
Delivered from the egg -
Apocalypse, with pellets full of bones.

BELLBINE

Curse to the farmer
And the gardener alike,
The convolvulus
Has few friends.

That their white bells
Hang from the
hedgerows in July,
Or their smaller cousins
Pinken over land -
In-filled with stars
And dusted by the sun;

Is not enough
To counter the demise
That comes with spades
And creosote and acid.

Yet I would raise a dais
To their flowers -
Sing paeans
To their beauty;

Would join the loud
Te Deum of the bees
And enter the
Communion of summer.

FOX CUB

Far more suspicious than surprised,
           confronted by my human image:
Two eyes that rouse my sentimental self -
That place this other creature, wreathed in flowers,
In some small world of story-books and fable.

I'll never know what cowers in that brain -
What fears there are, if fears as known exist;
Perceptions that divide us, unexplained -
           that leave us to our habitats of cunning.

He wanders off with others of his kind,
Beneath the hedge, where shadows run to earth;
Those tiny gloves of legend left behind
           to taint the verse, with words, like digitalis.

MATINEE

In May, when the days that lengthen
Stage the performance of their yearly pageant -

When the last rehearsal, free from the prompter
           and embarrassed silence,
Turns through its verses to the birds in chorus;

You can hear the doves with their wings applauding -
Where the gold laburnum fizzes like fire
Through the smoke of lilac and the weight of blossom
Dresses the hedgerows with a virgin whiteness;

You can hear the colour of a thousand words
Speak from the gardens on the lips of flowers -
Hear the sun's recital to the turning earth,
Hour by hour with the bees declaiming.

HUNTERS

We knew
    where the
        jackdaws nested -
Where the floor-joist
Rested on decaying brick
And our tested nerves
Shook to the edges of abysmal balance.

We knew
    where the
        mortar crumbled -
Where the Flemish-bond
Tumbled its brickwork
In a fall of dust
And our fumbled hands
Clawed at the entrance
        of a straw-filled chimney.

We saw
    where the
        nestlings huddled -
Where the sky's light
Puddled in the pools of soot
And where our muddled motives
Shook to the treble of their gaping mouths.

ST. BENET'S SHEEP

If you go to St.Benets, or is it Benedicts?
Where the old, red mill
Grows from the arches of the abbey's ruins;

You may, as I, a stranger on this road,
Whose dusty way is lined with Norfolk reeds,
Be slow at first, to hear the voice of prayer
That leaves the wind and feathers through the marsh;

But if you stand and stare across the Bure,
Where sails, in supplication, search the sky
And harriers hang cruciform on air;

You may, just once, be conscious in a while
Of how the past in plainsong lingers there
And why the geese in gaggles crop the sward.

ULTING CHURCH

Travel to Ulting church:
Take time to wander by the navigation -

See sky unravelled into twin description
As terns float upwards to concentric impact.

Ponder on willows that are air enacted -
That are words deciphered of the weather's cryptic.

Walk through the shadows into sun deflected -
Into light made liquid under green mosaic.

DECEMBER HUNT

After the hounds
and the horses
the water is cloudy.

The scent is lost
and the day drowns
in its own darkness.

A scarlet cloak
stands out
across the fields

and the fox
lies safely
in some distant cover.

Rooks and the first stars
reveal themselves
as opposites at dusk

and the moon
like a silver stirrup
curves through the heavens
with the earth in harness.

CHALLENGE

An abundance of berries:
Burden or bounty, it's hard to say -
The hedgerows sagging with the weight of summer.

The rowan is a witch's curse -
Heavy with portents of the coming season.

The fieldfares have no eye for beauty,
To them the may-tree is a feast -
Blood in the plunder of their own survival.

The rose-hip, but a ghost -
A red memento of a mortal flower.

The holly's eyes are manic in the shadows -
The sacred king uneasy in his crown.

LATE SEPTEMBER

The leaves half
green half yellow
and those that fall
like butterflies in swarms.

An invisible flail
threshes the river -
cuts grain in glass.

Three types of cloud
and plovers in the fields -
the swallows, out of nowhere,
    like a squall.

GAMES MASTER

Thank you Mr. Morgan for doing what you have to:
the woodbines are not very good for me -
I know I shouldn't smoke, especially in assembly.

I have no right to choke my classmates -
to stub my dog-ends on the parquet flooring.

Why should the headmaster suffer?
It's hard enough leading the rabble in prayer
without the ghost of my disgusting habit
climbing the hairs up the holes in his nose
and making him splutter through the Latin verses.

Thank you Mr. Morgan for your chapel sentiments:
I note the fist on the back of the head -
the ringing in the ears, the rattle of teeth.

It's such a relief to be so forgiven -
to pay a ransom for one's sins.

I've always admired the Welsh -
such wonderful teachers.

Mr. Roberts is the same,
a perfect shot with the blackboard rubber -
a first-class educationalist.

I'll see you both in the pub when I'm older -
we can talk about sex and socialism.

For now I'll get my kicks where I can -
behind the bike-shed, in the line-out or the scrum.

Thanks for the lesson in applied athletics -
I'll never forget the bum-fluff and the bullshit.

GRANDFATHER

He lived behind the Daily Herald,
a roll-up in his hands, tapers for the fire.

He was a master in the art of silence;
the token word, the subtle gesture.

Surprising, how he changed at Christmas
    the cockney Saturnalia.

The role-reversal seemed to suit him,
the lipstick and the license of misrule,
the rustle of his petticoats, the wig.

Just once a year he acted out the fool -
played the piano, danced and sang,
told stories to the children.

Later, when he started wandering,
still shell-shocked by the world about him,
we children found him difficult to follow.

We couldn't understand; the ramblings,
    the war-talk.

When the police brought him back,
cold from an all-night sortie,
    he never spoke.

They buried him in ground not far from home;
one final trench, his prophecy fulfilled.

EXTRA! EXTRA!

PAPER! EVENING PAPER!

Ship sinks in Channel
   all drowned.

READ ALL ABOUT IT!

PAPER! EVENING PAPER!

Plane crash in London
   no survivors.

READ ALL ABOUT IT!

PAPER! EVENING PAPER!

Motorway pile-up
   dozens
killed and injured.

READ ALL ABOUT IT!

PAPER! EVENING PAPER!

Poet writes a poem
   about spring -
case continues.

EXTRA! EXTRA!

READ ALL ABOUT IT!

PAPER! EVENING PAPER!

VIOLETS

Shrinking to a speck of colour -
a pinch of sweetness.

I find you by the woodland paths -
hidden in grasses,

Like miniature purple-emperors
Waiting for the oaks to flourish.

You are at one with the shadows -
secretive, mysterious.

You wear your Lenten vestments like a priest
And on my knees I venerate your shrine.

GATHERING HOLLY

We are the last to get to the holly,
What berries there are, are right at the top.

December keeps up with tradition,
Lashes of rain, clouds at the gallop.

Heads down we blunder through the thicket
Until we find some berries we can reach.

I hold you steady on the bank
As you snip away with your secateurs.

Each year, the same place, the same weather,
Nothing like the cards, the deep snow, the icicles.

We still enjoy it though, the ritual,
The evergreen enchantment that it brings.

A robin tries its hardest oblige -
Appears on cue, and sings at centre-stage.

I look at you and you return the glance,
What words there are, are better left unsaid.

WILDERNESS

When you watch them; really watch them -
The snake with dislocated jaws
    swallowing the lizard;

Or the paralysing wasp
Using the spider as a neat for eggs;
It is hard not to fail the test -

    not to think of love
As anything but paragraphs of text
Written by madmen with a thirst for deserts.

GREAT TIT

When I think of spring,
I hear the repetitions of its song -
The tinny, two-note treble that it flings
From tree to tree, still leafless after winter.

And when I hear, I know it won't be long
Before the bud-scales scatter to the street
And turn the year to flutterings of greenness.

And yet I fear the heat is far too strong -
With time enough for things to turn severe
And catch a pond's reflections unawares.

But still it rings its clear, contentious call
From tree to tree, unruffled by my thoughts -
Its yellow breast expanding to the thrall
Of life expressed eternally as echoes.

THE SAWYER'S TALE

When I worked in the sawmill
They gave us a pint of milk a day -
Some say it was generous, others were not so sure;
    It was a grand life though -
        Gave you a buzz -
        Understand?
We had some laughs, me and the lads,
Mucking about in the sawdust, throwing chippings;
The work was hard, we didn't mind though,
    Friday-night was coming -
        Bit of a bonus,
        Few extra beers,
        No sweat!
That day old Ted cut his finger though,
Something else, right to the bone it was -
Stuck it in the band-saw, didn't have the guard up,
        Know what I mean?
He didn't complain though,
Wrapped it in an old rag, carried on working;
We told him to put it in the accident book,
He didn't bother, said he'd be alright -
        Tough old stick,
        War veteran,
    Bit of a hard-nut in his time,
        Savvy?
Well, it went septic, had to have his arm off,
Couldn't work no more; still he was near retirement -
They gave him a good send-off, rare old party it was;
He seemed happy with the gold watch -
Me and the lads had a whip-round,
        Give him a few extra quid,
        No sweat!
That's what it was like in those days,
Help each other out, look after your muckers -
He had a bit of a pension coming,
        He'd be alright,
        Understand?
We had our own lives to live, work to do, money to earn;
They still gave us a pint of milk a day -
Some say it was generous, others weren't so sure;
    I left there in the end, joined the army, wanted a trade,

Something for the future; you've got to move on -
    You know, get some in,
      Know what I mean?
As it happens, I didn't do too well in the army,
Would have been alright, but for the accident -
Still, luck of the draw; probably get a little pension;
Can't complain, there's always someone worse-off
        than you:
     Know what I mean -
        Savvy?

CHELMER VALLEY

There are wilder woods than these -
Rivers, whose courses
Cleave from the sheer rocks -
Thunder through chasms.

There are lusher meadows:
Meanders looping into lakes -
Willows more willowy.

The mistakes are mine:
Eyes too full of memory -
Tears too sentimental.

The fallacy remains:
Trees are gestures -
Flowers, words
Translated into fragrance.

I cannot help but
Read the wings of swallows -
Hear voices at the weir's edge -
Decipher clouds.

The code is broken:
The rain weeps -
The earth responds.

Grasses whisper:
Seeds speak -
Leaves interpret.

The spoken world
Is written in the water -
Renamed and resonant.

Vibrations reach a pitch
Too sharp for sound -
A dragonfly drops stitches
Draws a thread.

STARLING

Master of mimics
Out of clicks
And murmurs.

Street-curlew -
Phone-caller -
Ghost at the corner
Of contrary skies -
Hawking the habit
Of its clone acoustics.

Slang-shuffler -
Kerb-coster -
Hunching its shoulders
To the inch of hustle.

Spiv in the market
Of plebian sparrows -
Touting the traffic
Of its sway and swagger.

Crowd-pusher -
Beak-stabber -
Shifty in winter
With a bib of blizzards -
Slick into summer
With its suit a spectrum.

THE BACK-PATH

Along the path between the hedges and the tall trees:
the smell of humus in the ditch -
grass in tufts brimming from the flood.

Here, where all autumns are as one -
fermenting fruit, brambles a bounty.

She stands, holding the corners of her apron -
he, loading the windfalls, smiles.

They are used to endeavour, water from the well,
logs and kindling, oil for the lamps.

We, children from a bombed-out city -
eyes dilated, like a crop of sloes:
every step a miracle, and we the chosen people.

CAT
For years you've used my step
And still you do not trust me.

The colour of clouds
You evaporate at will.

I try to encourage you:
Make noises with my lips -

Clickings with my tongue.
You do not respond

Other than to disappear round corners.
You seem made of air:

Grey as a mist -
Nearly invisible.

You twist through your own pelt -
An artist with the essence of escape.

I try once more to capture your consent
But then you melt, like shadows in the rain.

CANADA GEESE

The Canadas are feeding on the wheat -
When evening comes they'll rise above the fields
And beat the bounds of autumn with their wings.

They'll draw their threads of sound across the sky
Like signatures, half-written by the wind
That sighs through trees and scatters tears of gold.

On frosted air they'll slide towards their roost,
Like angels down an elemental stair
To prove themselves the deities of ice.

THE FALCONER

It could have been any age:
The man with a buzzard on his arm -
The church and the river.

He could have been a knight
    or a prince -
Chasing the hare, the rabbit.

The buzzard, came to his whistle
    like a dog:
Flew from the tree -
Greeted his arm with talons.

The excitements are the same -
Though tinged with guilt.

I wanted to see the quarry
    and the kill:
The grace at wing, the aerobatics.

I wanted to see the hare across the fields:
The twist and turn of feather over fur -
    the skill surviving.

CROCUSES

When I see the yellow crocuses
I think of the beaks of birds -
Of nestlings gaping for their food;

　　In fact
I shouldn't be surprised
If they began to chirp -
If they proved me right
And hopped across the lawn.

COINCIDENCE

　　I saw them together -
The kingfisher and the white blackbird.

They seemed exotic in that place -
The water-splash in flood, the leafless trees.

That it should happen in the rain was uplifting -
The sky a shade less grey, the season warmer.

They flew away and disappeared upstream -
The water-splash still ruffled by their absence.

HOMESTEADER

We used to drive his old jalopies -
over the fields, the unmade roads.

Get in a rut and you'd stay there,
like a needle in a groove.

We played the same tunes every week:
gangsters on the running-boards -

Fangio behind the wheel.
They say he was backward:

preferred the company of children -
enjoyed their games.

He didn't seem silly to me,
not when he gave us sweets, money.

His two old aunts kept ducks and chickens:
we used to steal their eggs -

cook them on the camp fire.
Once, we took his bicycle -

sold it to the gypsies.
He never knew it was us:

still played our games -
forked out for friendship.

BLANK

There is nothing
but the snow
to write about.

The river is frozen
unwilling
to release an image.

Trees are leafless
birds without song.

I add my tracks
to the others
and wander off
a partner
to the silence.

The sky is monotone
a grey weight
heavy
with the thoughts
of crystal.

A few loose flakes
stutter
in the evening air
then are lost.

A pheasant
breaks the stillness
and the calm.

Struts out
across the night's
unwritten pages.

SONG

Along the railway path
there's a line of trees.
Just before dark
when the breezes sigh
    their last

and the earth is crossed
in sunlight and in shadow -
high from out a fretwork
    made of leaves

a thrush imparts
its lonely evening song.
I scarce believe
the poignancy it brings -

how grief is told
on each repeated phrase
and how the song
    delimits all to dusk.

LATE MARCH

This is a day for the swallows:
late March, the bees
about their business -

the butterflies commuting.
The sun shows a profit -
the books are balanced

with light to spare.
Only the tulips are in the red
and even they seem careless.

IN THE WOODS

This year all things
have bloomed together,
anemones and sorrel,

stitchwort and bluebells.
More like August than April,
the weather warm,

the air so humid.
A yaffle laughs
in the woods

and the jays are raucous.
I walk through flowers,
as on water,

blue sea, white waves.
The sun moves
through the branches

like a golden fish.
I take a breath
and dive into the shadows.

CHANGEABLE

The lilac and laburnum
   Start to grow
Where the wind has turned the weather
Into snow and ice together
And the swallow keeps its feathers
   Flying low.

This is not the way that summer
   Means to take
Where the celandine are sneezes
In the ditches as it freezes
And the petals in the breezes
   Fail to wake.

The spring is getting colder
   I believe
Where the migrants know the traces
Of the cherubs puffing faces
And the winter pulls the aces
   From its sleeve.

ON DAYS

On days like these -
When the blackbird sings
And the bees are a burden
            in the throats of flowers.

When the first real warmth
Opens a curtain in the depth of cloud
And the gold laburnum tempers the lilac
            and the backs of swallows.

On days like now -
When the thought that follows
Climbs with the skylark into pools of air -
Drowns in the heavens like a blue devotion.

SPRING HATCH

There's been a hatch of flies:
small, like winter gnats -
the air is thick with them.

They rise and fall in
　misty spirals:
smoke without fire -
substance without form.

I try to avoid them
but they catch in the hair
and irritate the skin.

　Back to back
they consummate their being:
love conquers all -
even the food for swallows.

DOUBLE-TAKE

A fleck of yellow drifts across the eye
And then becomes a brimstone butterfly.

Across the lawn a whiteness waddles on
To prove again how graceless is the swan;

And in the air a swallow skims the lake
Where one is two in water's double-take.

CRICKET BAT WILLOWS

I was watching them cut the willows -
Trees that I remember being planted.

No more will their reflections delve the river -
No chance collusion with the banks of cloud.

They are dragging them out with a tractor -
Lopping the branches with a chain-saw.

When somebody scores a century
And lifts his bat to acknowledge the applause;

Will anyone think of the river as it was -
Before the wind had lost the willow's voice?

ONCE

The children walk down to the stream:
naked as the sun's rays -
gilded with innocence.

They wade above their own reflections:
their spirit image -
blurred and ghostlike.

Not a bird sings in the August heat:
songs are the insects' world -
the bees, the crickets.

The stream ripples in the breeze:
and the children's laughter -
teases the senses.

Memory is all that's left:
the passing light -
transparencies and shadows.

WORDS FOR AUTUMN

Autumn poems are the best -
Poems when the year is at the turn
And words are blest like leaves across the wind.

Time for the bramble and the wasp -
When morning fields are spidery and wet
And breath is lost like ghosts upon the air.

A place where the fruits are ripe -
Where the blackthorn holds each berry with a bloom
That chooses light dissolving into mist.

A sky, September blue -
Where geese that fly in loose unwritten lines
Decry the news of winter in their wake.

FOG

    November's eye is closing -
The things that were no longer hold their shape
And half the sky is blinded by the fog.

Across the lake a pair of swans dissolve -
Their mute perfection worried to a grey similitude;
Leaves, like unwanted words, waste on the silent air
And all that was is otherwise related.

WILLOW CUTTING

More like autumn than summer:
The men, cutting willows -
Burning branches.

Smoke lies thick across the river:
The wheat-fields, gold -
The distance, bluish.

I watch the moorhens in the shallows:
Ticking like clockwork -
Heads, nodding.

The terns are on patrol:
Hovering an instant -
Dipping to their own reflections.

Swallows will soon be gathering:
Swifts already gone -
The cuckoo, also.

Spiderlings are lofted by the breeze:
Rise on a thermal -
Await their dispersals.

Soon the geese in gaggles will return:
Skeins on a blue glaze -
Cracks in the pattern.

MOMENTS

1.
As I brush
Past the privet
The collected rain
Spatters my clothing.

If it wasn't
For the smell
Of cut grass
I would be angry.

2.
Sometimes I pick
A rose petal -
Place it between
Finger and thumb
And squeeze it
For its fragrance.

If the rose
Knew that I
Was coming:
That my motives
Were not honourable -
Could I escape the thorns?

3.
At night by
The scented stocks
The moths seem
Almost intoxicated.

I put my hands
In amongst them
And stagger at
The touch of wings.

4.
I've been rubbing
Out the eggs
On the backs
Of cabbage leaves.

Does this mean
I prefer cabbage
To butterflies?

5.
Every day as I
Walk along the path
The spiders' webs
Break across my face.

If I were a spider
Would I learn
From my mistakes?

6.
Dahlias and
Chrysanthemums
Were his favourite flowers.

She also learnt to love them.

    When I see them cut
  they look
Funereal.

7.
The leaves
Fall into
The gutter
And float
Away, like
Paper boats.

The chosen
  one
Is scuttled
By a twig.

8.
The fruit trees
Are at their best.

Apples and plums
  are strewn
Across the grass.

Starlings and wasps -
The only weather.

9.
The lawn whitens
In the frost
And the bird-bath
Freezes over.

The ground
Is harder now:
The breath a ghost -
The branches bone-like.

10.
We are waiting
For the first snow.

Silence and coldness
The indications -
The cloud miserly.

11.
I fill the bucket
From the coal-bunker.

The shovel scrapes
On the concrete.

The sound of winter.

12.
The garden
Softens
Under snow.

The early
Growth
Is ready.

The sun
Ascendant.

13.
The crocuses
Are through:

Like the
Gapes of birds -

Hungry for sunlight.

14.

The pear tree's
In blossom.

The petals
Fall in the wind
Like confetti.

The bees
Are the
Bridesmaids.

15.
The hedgerows
Are greener now.

The Queen-Anne's-lace
Adds whiteness as a contrast.

The rain - its musk.

16.
I look for the swifts -
When they come
It will be summer.

They are the
Air described:
Dark thermals -
Obsidian starlight.

1991-1995

DEATH SLIDE

There's something unutterably English
about a town-show. It goes without saying
that the weather will be doubtful. To wish

for anything else would in its own way
be almost foreign. We prefer the clouds,
the stoic resignation to the rain.

The arts-and-crafts, a refuge for the crowds,
who dampened but undaunted in marquees
stand back to gauge perspectives, stilted flowers.

Portraits from photographs, calligraphy,
these are the things that label it worthwhile.
Style doesn't matter; origami,

bonsai, wine from local vineyards, piles
of books sold with a charitable zeal,
all have their place, despite the urge to smile.

There's something intrinsically unreal
about it, like the dogs in the arena
jumping through hoops of fire. One might feel

the death-slide, manned by the 2nd Para,
incongruous enough; but these girls
in summer clothes, diagonal enigmas

through the air, suspended here in worlds
of youthful bluff; elate, uncultured pearls.

SPIRITS

I like a drop of rum:
Caribbean sunshine -
distilled and bottled;

the idea of pirates:
those swashbuckling types -
gold earrings, teeth, doubloons;

the romance of it all:
the off-the-shoulder serving wenches -
adventurous eyes, cleavage.

I don't think much about sugar:
the cane-fields, molasses,
    dunder;

my mind's a map:
footprints over silver sand -
palm-trees, coral;

as for the darker trade:
that message from the commerce of the sea -
X - marks the spot.

WINDY DAY

A crow, tired of its heavy flight,
Slipped out across diagonals of air
And vanished in the wizardry of branches.

The sun, with its own brief magic,
Regained a sudden fraction of the sky
Then faded like the yellowing of paper,

A conjuror, who wasn't even there,
Turned every held umbrella inside-out
With just a breath, and nothing up his sleeve.

SNOW PIECE

At Barling Magna, across the fields of snow,
   with the evening sun
      red in the fire of returning frost;

I saw the rooks fly low across the ground,
Like living art distilled from pen and ink
      to counteract the whiteness of the page;

And there without the hook of any sound
I heard the written phoneme of a star
      expound the brittle languages of ice.

A DAY IN MARCH

  You know the warmth I mean -
That time of year, when winter, though not passed,
Is not so keen to carve its name in ice.

When every stem, as if a tube of glass,
Allows the sap, like temperature, to rise
And reach the golden centigrade of flowers.

That touch of heat, as tentative as song,
That blossoms on the boughs of disbelief
And rights the wrong of silence under snow.

NEW MOON

This evening, an unlucky one for brides:
The may tree white with blossom
And the Queen-Anne's-lace
Ghosting the shadows and the dew-wet grasses -

We two, too old for superstition,
Beneath a moon we'd never see through glass,
Turn over coins and make our separate wishes;

And in the ash, just coming into leaf,
We find our hopes redoubled by a thrush,
Whose sole belief is wedded to a song.

BARN OWL

I saw a barn owl the other night:
Like a big, white moth
Riding the air-waves
Of our urban darkness.

It fluttered around the streetlamps:
Its blunt, unblinking face
Turning from side to side -
Its wings, a silence.

Strange to see it in town:
A country cousin,
Up for the day,
Quartering the market.

I am fearful of its commerce:
Its trade in fur and feather -
Its large, cold eyes,
Angled for bargains.

TURBULENCE

Like fallen clouds
the blackthorns billow -
thicken with blossom.

A cumulus landscape:
adrift on an April breeze -
floating in the sky's blue ocean.

The winter wheat
crests in a green wave -
ripples with silver.

A church like a grey ship
plunges through a tide of grass -
founders on gravestones.

Rooks at the top of trees:
ride out the swell -
are slick with mutiny.

SONG THRUSH

The ash is feathery with flowers
Where the thrush astounds us
With its April music.

How many hours must it sing
Before the task
Of boundaries is over?

I cannot ask it:
We sing a different tune -
Confuse our meanings.

Truth - beauty : beauty - truth,
Whatever, there is time enough for song,
Albeit that the song has other ends.

Sing thrush! Sing!
Confound us with the rhythms of your needs -
Allow us yet the measure of illusion.

MARCH MORNING

This morning was another place -
Each blade of grass was bristling with frost
And every tree a ghost against the blue.

The fishpond was a white, obscuring glass
Allowing neither light nor any view
To pass beyond the censor of itself.

A chaffinch flew from branch to dipping branch
As if a spark was kindled out of ice
To chance the air made steamy by the sun;

And everywhere, the rumor that was spring,
Was echoed by the blackbird and the thrush;
Until by noon the world had had enough
Of winter and its crystalline attire.

SINGULARITY

It's difficult to think of nothing -
if not impossible

wherever the mind goes
there's always space
if only notional

even here in the fog
far from land
the mudflats soft underfoot
is still somewhere

but it has the look of nothing
if you'll excuse the contradiction

grey is the only colour
a sort of cold neutrality

there are sounds of suction
the smell of seaweed
dank autumnal air

a pair of redshank
veer in from nowhere
pass either side
with pipings of alarm

it's almost timeless
save heart and breath
the memory of sequence

a curlew's voice
enumerates the marsh
each haunted word
dimensionless, like zero.

TALKING TO THE BEES

What to do when a friend goes mad -
When the head lets loose its fragments like a swarm
And every sting is barbed to pump its venom -
When the wings of words, fan at the hive's lip,
And dance the dance of convolute direction?
What comb within the frenzy that surrounds
Will ever drip the sweetness it deserves
When every cell is shrouded under wax?

I am no keeper of the bees:
I turn away from urges that react -
That leave the air cacophonous with anger.

Behind the veil I watch the flameless smoke,
And though I talk, the bees are still disturbed -
Will not accept the mask of my composure.

NEVERTHELESS THROUGH GRASSES

Saying that the sun speaks
that its words are waves
decipherable
in peaks
and troughs
and distances
is helpful if the eyes
are cut like prisms
if our religion
is divisible from whiteness
and the rainbow bends
through definite degrees -
when the lark is infinity
or almost
a pencil-point
a full-stop
for its own song
then our differences
are air and gravity
are longings
for the impossible

nevertheless through grasses
where the adder curves
where the burnet-moth
and the skipper
stir through the shimmers
of incessant heat
and the ranunculus
like butter
bleats its pathetic pollen -
then is it reasonable to ask
then when the tongue
like the swallow's tail
forks over summer
with its sweet surmisals
when the bee beats
on incredulous wings
and the moon like honey
climbs the horizon
of our dark misgivings.

HUMBUG

Well I'm sick of it, I can tell you;
All the way from the North Pole
Upwind of eight reindeer.

Snow, sleet, frost, fog,
I don't know, what do I do it for?

You try parking a sleigh on the roof -
Tiptoeing along the ridge-tiles
With a hundredweight of nuts and oranges.

What do they think I'm made of, elastic?
Chimney after chimney, hot ash, soot, cinders;
Mountains of mince-pies, an ocean of sherry.

None of them are worth it; mindless brats:
Spend all year pulling the wings off flies -
    picking their noses.

Now, all of a sudden; it's dear Santa,
Would you, could you, will you, can I?

Herod had the right idea:
I've half a mind to fill their socks with arsenic -
Suffocate the cherubs where they sleep.

Bring back Saturnalia, that's what I say -
    not a virgin to be seen
And Balthazar, blind stupid on the vino.

JACKSON'S POND

Ducks on a pond
and five geese cropping the sward.
What does it mean:

this signal from the yellow-flags -
the lily-pads
like palms in supplication?

The last of the chestnut-candles,
scatter their wax -
dowse in their own reflections.

Is it a dream -
the same old vision
fathoming the mirror?

The cloudscapes
with the swallows in-between -
fish like shadows

floating in a green suspension.
Where am I -
is summer a place or a thought?

This is real enough:
the sheen across clear glass -
the mood transparent.

A feather
like a crescent-moon
drifts on the air's breath:

the sun
a burning question in the west -
the light eclipsing.

PLOTLANDERS

Built before the war as weekend cottages
They soon became a refuge for the homeless -
The bombed-out, blitzed-out, many.

Cottages? a euphemism really:
Four-square on brick-piers, timber-framed,
Asbestos-walls, roofs of corrugated-iron.

When the fighting stopped; some stayed on,
Tried to make a go of it. No picnic though:
Chickens and geese, a plot for spuds and cabbages,

Well-water. Years later, when I was in my teens,
I used to visit Mrs Pappworthy;
Eighty-odd, crippled, but still surviving.

Alterations were her stock-in-trade: coats,
Shirts, trousers; you name it, she could fix it.
"Come in lad, git yer pants off, sit yerself dahn."

So, there I sat, goose-fleshed and well embarrassed.
Inside, it was dark and dank, the smell of cats,
Mildew. A long-case clock chimed through the quarters,

As light through a netted-window,
Gave her the look of a work by Rembrandt.
I gazed around at the souvenirs:

Ashtrays from Margate and Clacton, china-dogs
Won at the fair, bits of brass, candlesticks, thimbles.
On the mantle-shelf, between chromium vases,

A sepia-photograph ghosted the room.
'Who's that,' I said, thoughtlessly, as she licked
The end of her cotton-thread. "It's me ol' man, ducks,"

She muttered, "been dead these ten years." You know
How it is when you wish you hadn't spoken;
Everything went silent, except, that is, for the clock.

CASUALTY

The smooth-snake, rare
        yet unprotected
                from the traffic.

              A six-inch gash
      in its stomach, viscera
Spilling out.
Writhing, but stationary:
        its muscles severed -
            a wave, that wavers.
        "What can we do?" she said,
"We can't just leave it."
So I cut its head off,
            there at the side of the road:
    watched its mouth contort -
Its jaws dislocate.
I left it by the verge -
           food for the crows, no doubt;
        they've learnt the necessary trick:
    can dodge the cars -
The pitying, the guilt.

GENESIS

When you're out and about at the end of April:
One of those days of sunshine and of shadow -
   Rain and rainbows.

When the primrose clumps are clustered by the verge
   And the violets, a fragrance
      Interspersing.

   How much a miracle it is:
   Walking over green waves
Between the moving patterns of the clouds -
     The golden spaces.

     High up
   And the lark in stasis:
   Hanging on its own song -
  Phrases in the literatures of light.

When you're out and about at the end of April
One of those days of warmth and winter -
   Hail and thunder.

When the edges of the world are sharp-defined
   And the distances, outspoken,
      Underlining.

   How much and magical it is:
    To see the weather's wand
Waving through the labyrinths of leaves -
     Across the ponds.

     High up
   And the lark still singing:
   Hanging on its every phrase -
  Belonging to the languages of sky.

UNREQUITED

I know what they're up to, horrible brats;
    think I'm a witch, you see,
        come round here to frighten themselves.
Look at that one -
    the one with the blue eyes, blond hair;
        have you ever seen such an angelic face?
He's the worst of the lot,
    always trying to prove something -
        always at the front, calling me names, swearing.
He's the last to leave as well,
    dancing around, taunting me,
        pretending he's not scared.
Watch him, when he's back among his friends -
    out of range, safe beyond the garden,
        out there in the alley.
See how he struts and swaggers;
    you'd think he was brave, wouldn't you?
        his friends do, he's fooled them, at least.
I know what he's up to; I've been watching
    kids for years, wanted them myself once -
        if it hadn't been for mother, god rest her, dear mother.
Still, I've got my cats, they love me. He's back again, listen!
    "Come out you old bat! You old hag!
        Cast a spell, give us curse."
If only he knew,
    what I wouldn't do for some magic -
        the power of words, the gift of transformation.
Look at him, what a beautiful child -
    those blue eyes, that blond hair,
        the way he moves, the arrogance, the bravado.
I know what he's up to poor mite:
    oh mother, dear mother,
        puss! puss! puss! come to mummy, mummy loves you.

ROUGH GRAINED

Almost spherical:
a short, fat, red-faced little man -
thin-lipped and bitter.

A woodyard, he called it, that derelict plot:
heaps of rubble, scrap-iron, rickety sheds.

How he hated us kids:
"Piss-off, you scruffy oiks,
I've got enough on me plate
without you bastards prattin' about."

Nobody liked him:
how he made a living with junk-wood
and a clapped-out old truck;
none could fathom.

Rumour was rife, of course -
all sorts of dubious dealings
invented on his behalf.

He kept bull-terriers -
squat and mean,
just like their master.

Once, for a joke, we went to buy some timber:
"Timba," he yelled, "I'll give yer timba,"
flaying about with a length of tongue-and-groove -

his terriers, no underdogs; all teeth,
as one by one we dovetailed through the hedge.

CHANGING TENSE

When summer came, we used to go carp fishing:
Nothing serious, makeshift tackle, sandwiches, a bottle of pop.

    We were after crucians:
    small, but powerful -
    six inches of golden muscle.

    The willow pond, we called it:
    waist-deep at most -
    covered in crowsfoot, lilies.

It could have been the Amazon:
              dragonflies; blue-green metallic -
                      hovered, like humming-birds.

The grass snake; a diminutive anaconda.

    The swims were few:
    rifts of open water -
    drinking sky, cloud gathering.

    Mesmerized, I sat
    watching the cork -
    tuned to its every tremor.

My thoughts were of leviathan:
Monsters, with scales the size of saucers -
Great rubbery lips, barbules, like twists of rope.

What if I fell in? If the piranhas got me?

Would I be pared to the bone, a skeleton;
              only discovered in a drought -
                      bleaching in the tropic heat?

I took another swig of lemonade -
        a cuckoo, made derisory remarks,
                and from the reeds, a whisper, or a sigh.

SOME HOPE

No-one here thinks they're Napoleon -
   Let alone Josephine.

The schizophrenics - plagued by persecutors -
Suffer the same old jokes -
   The double entendre.

The manic - swing on their own tides:
   Buoyant or aground -
Subject to the mind's inclemency.

Me - one of the neurotics:
Chlorpromazine a force field round the bed -
   Pandora's box;
The head's enduring fragments.

RELLA'S

When I worked at the market -
I felt important.

You know how it is for a kid -
Earning money, feeling grown up.

Six in the morning, unloading vans -
Setting-up the stalls.

I was so proud of it -
Chest out, bit of a swagger.

"Leave it to me," I'd say, "I'll do it,
No bovver."

I helped out on a clothes stall:
Children's wear, gear for the toddlers -
Baby schmutter.

I had a good line in chat, those days:
Was quick with the banter, the smart answer -
A right little tuck-up merchant.

Bespoke! Not a word of it -
"Ready-to-wear apparel," Rella said,
"Appeal to the snob in 'em."

"Beautiful baby missus, just like her muvver;
What about this? She'll look luvly in pink."

"It's a boy," she said, indignantly.
"Just testing luv!" I replied,
 "What side does 'e 'ang?" Laughter.......

CHAPTER AND VERSE

I never meant to steal it -
I wasn't even interested in books.

No, fear was the problem -
We had to pay for whatever we lost.

Was I to risk the headmaster:
His punishing looks -
The swish of retribution?

Or suffer my parents:
Their like severity -
Incarceration?

The decision was taken - literally -
    out of my hands:
Caught in the locker-room -
Erasing the name.

Would that the memory were so easy:
It was a wrong, admittedly -
But whose?

I offered my excuses, religiously:
Justice was unmitigated -
Six-of-the-worst; indelible.

EARLY CHAPTER

She meant a lot to me -
Though she didn't know it.

She worked on her father's stall -
Selling books; comics.

All I could do was look:
Too shy to talk -
Too young for the competition.

All the lads; strutting:
Slick with Brylcream -
Sloppy-Joes, tight trousers.

The choice was hers, she didn't bother -
Kept to herself; a first edition.

I'd thumb through the pages of the books:
Trying to appear knowledgeable -
An intellectual.

It made no difference though:
Comical - as ever - with the plot -
My lack of style; full-stops and no denouement.

LEARNING THE TRICKS

I remember my first bet -
Half-a-crown each way, I think.

I don't know the name of the horse:
'Loser's-Lad', 'Pinch-Pocket' -
What's the difference?
    It's still running.

It seemed to set a pattern to my life:
No matter how much I knew about form -
The content still eluded me.

I didn't want to be lucky in love:
Give me a full-house,
A prial of threes -
    Snap even!

The odds were against happy families -
A game of chance;
    Genetics.

As for nurture:
Too many knaves in the pack -
One-for-his-knob, at best.

Horses, dogs, cards; you name it:
A raw deal, the wrong track -
Always the clichés, never the winners.

When I learnt Solo,
I thought it'd all change -
Skill and chance combined; unity.

I should have known better:
The odds were stacked as usual -
I called abondance; but you've guessed,
    I made misère.

CHEERS!

Down at the club; nobody, talks war:
on the far wall - above the piano -
there's a painting of the Queen.

Between songs, we fill our glasses -
stock-up on lager; club-doubles.

Surrounded, by regimental badges:
pictures of ships; planes, tanks -
we mellow with the booze.

Most of the men have been in action -
care not to remember.

When the singing's done,
they play the National Anthem.

One of the men says, what's lager backwards?
we work it out……. laughter.

Another says, what about, royals?
we stand to attention -
habits, are addictive.

TOPSY-TURVY

Taciturn's an understatement:
my grandfather, was master of the grunt -
the impatient gesture.

The smell of 'Nut-Brown', all-pervasive:
    rolled-up tapers,
ripped from the 'Daily Herald' -
ready, for the pot-black stove.

"Don't tawk to 'im," granny said,
"mis'rable ol' sod, come ova 'ere
'av' a chat wiv me."

He wasn't always like it:
you should have seen him at Christmas -
a transformation.

Him and his brother:
dressed up as women -
doing the knees-up.

'Unda the table you must go,
ee-eye, ee-eye, ee-eye-o,
if I catch yer bendin'
I'll saw yer legs right off,
knees-up, knees-up,
don't fergit the breeze-up,
knees-up muvver brahn'.

So much make-up;
more like clowns than women:
uncanny really, chasing us kids
screaming all over the house.

When we picked the tree,
he'd dress-up as Santa Claus:
you could still smell the 'Nut-Brown' though -
something of a puzzle;
did they have tobacconists at the North Pole?

There were so many kids,
that dinner was in two sittings.

Turkey, goose, pork, rabbit:
saved-for all year -
scoffed in an instant.

My favourite, was Christmas pudding:
    every bite a lottery -
those silver-joeys: glistening - like tinsel.

IN ARREARS

After the cancer had been removed,
she seemed to be recovering -
until - septicemia - that is.

In intensive care,
she was given the last rites.

Later, back on the ward,
she said how kind the priest had been -
coming to see her; praying, she'd get better.

Fed and medicated by intravenous drips:
she lay there, feverish -
cooled by electric fans.

"If only I wasn't so hot," she 'd say,
"I could cope with almost anything,
any amount of pain; but this heat!"

She kept retching:
I held the sputum bowl to her mouth -
wiped her lips.

Probably the closest we'd ever been:
here on the cancer ward -
holding hands.

"Have you paid the rent, the gas,"
she said, "I've never been in arrears,
I'm not starting now."

Funny, what seems important -
even here.

I was at home when she died:
my brother came to tell me -
it seemed unreal, somehow.

When we collected her things:
her personal effects, as they called them -
I was affronted by the plastic bag.

Is this what life comes down to, I thought:
a few bits and pieces -
shampoo, soap, false-teeth.

So unprepared for keepsakes such as these -
pathos or bathos? I don't know;
the irony, eludes me.

BEING ORIGINAL

    When I joined the cubs,
I was asked what faith I belonged to -
How was I to know? I was only seven.

'I think I'm a Christian,' I said,
'Anyway, I go to church on Sunday
And we pray to somebody called God.'

"Are you a Protestant?" he persisted.

'No,' I replied, 'I don't think so;
I might be a Roman Catholic,
But I've never been to Rome.'

"Right!" he said, "when we say prayers,
You, can stand in the corner."

'But I haven't done anything wrong,' I complained,
'You only stand in the corner
      if you're naughty.'

"We're a C-of-E pack," he continued,
"We can't pray with Catholics; it's a sin."

'You could go to confession,' I said,
        innocently.......

A SWINGING MOOD

I'm shy, sensitive and insecure -
don't worry, this isn't a confessional poem;

I'd just like the critics and reviewers
to know of my neuroses in advance.

I want to discuss parties:
social ones, that is -
everything from the soiree to the booze-up.

In particular, I'm concerned about kitchens -
their magnetic properties.

Why is it, that those of us terrified of encounters elsewhere,
can communicate ten-deep over sinks and ovens?

'Hi there, what do you do?'
"oh, I'm on group therapy at the moment;"
'really, I haven't seen you at the clinic,
who's your consultant?'

The conversation turns to medicaments:
people, move in closer -
offer advice - relate experiences.

Fortified by rum and chlorpromazine
I decide to brave the lounge.

Three or four couples, cavort ridiculously -
reliving the twist, the mashed-potato.

When the music stops, I pluck up courage -
'hi there, what do you do?'

"oh, I'm a linguist actually," she says, I wince;
'and you?' I continue, talking to her partner,
"me, I'm a psychiatrist," he grins; "care to dance?"

FUMING

The fire-alarms are temperamental -
they go off anytime; screeching.

The woman along the corridor
burns joss-sticks;
someone else - toast.

I've bought a rope, just in case -
abseiling; my speciality.

The firemen are sick of us -
may charge for call-outs.

I practice holding my breath -
walking, in the dark.

They've gone-off again -
I check the landing; sniff the air.

Back in the flat, I cover my head
with cushions; muffle the pitch.

Eventually, they stop -
the silence; smoulders.

I thumb, some rubbed tobacco
from my palm; ignite a match -
fume in a blue fug.

LUXEMBOURG

You know what it's like,
hardly a word of French
and not much acting ability.

"Bonjour madame, avez vous saucisson
avec les frites, s'il vous plait?"

She answers.......

"Pardon madame? je suis anglais,
il fait tres beau temps."

'I English a little,' she replies,
'what you want very much?'

"Sausage, worst; chips, pomme-frits."
I mimic ludicrously.
'we have not sausages mister,
but chips we have many of.'

"Tres bon, mademoiselle," she blushes,
"pardon madam, je suis fou anglaise."

Giggles...

I try again, "jambon, s'il vous plait?"
'confiture?' she queries.

"Not to worry," I say,
"I'll settle for a Luxembourger!"
'Mais oui,' she says, 'Macdonalds.'

"Merci madame, auf wiedersehen."
'Danke schon, monsieur; bon appetite!'

SACRIFICE

While the church was being built
we used the footings
as a battle-field.

The ground - already consecrated -
was a series of earthworks.

Well entrenched;
we checked our weaponry:

air rifles, catapults, stones -
tooled-up for anything.

I crept out for a reckee -
clutching a brick,
behind the spoil-heap.

I could hear the enemy:
making plans -crawling towards us.

I pulled the pin, counted three,
and lobbed the grenade.......

When I heard the scream,
I was scared -
the excitement, left me.

I climbed to the top of the mound
and peered out across the soil.

A boy, head in hands,
stood in the altar-space -
blood, spouting.

PRECINCT

In the precinct, there are raised-beds -
oases of flowers.

Whatever the season, colour insinuates -
blooms, regardless.

Shoppers with green-fingers, stop to admire -
nod, knowingly.

The aged - in rows - along the benches:
   re-gather their strength -
      disseminate wisdom.

Pigeons, like grey seed:
   scatter from fractious children -
      are blown, like petals.

PARTY POLITICAL BROADCAST CIRCA 1492

I'm the same age as the president
of the United States of America.

What this means in real terms:
in the final analysis -
is a good question.

With the right P.R. man -
a different accent
and the governorship of Arkansas;

I could have been as great as him,
and he, could have been the author
of this - very minor - poem.

Columbus, on the other hand,
not wishing to be either, I presume,
settled for seamanship and voyages of discovery.

Politics, being what they were, even then,
he persuaded his backers that Panama and the Orinoco
were somewhere close to Bombay and Calcutta;

and rumour has it, that this is why we're told,
that although black-holes are there, we cannot see them,
and that Bombay ducks; are fish!

PITHECANTHROPUS

When I walk round the supermarket,
I am minded of the apes.

Not that the cashier has hairy knuckles,
or the security guard a low forehead;

it's just, when I look at the cans,
I wonder how we used to manage.

It's okay coming down from the trees,
But what can you do without a tin-opener?

I know it's easy to be glib on a full stomach,
    but think of it -
what would we do without the frozen chicken?

Where does carbohydrate come from -
how many kilos of roots and grass must you eat,
    just to stay alive?

Are chickens born in polythene:
do chips grow on trees -
is money - really - made of plastic?

These are the questions I ask -
not to be flippant, you understand.

I'm well aware of the dialectical response -
cheap food, leisure time, progress.

It's just, when I see them carrying their bags:
arms full-stretch - loping along the street -
it's the banana-skins, that worry me.

WATCHING THE GAME

Why do I watch the game?
I don't even know the rules.

Blame it on tradition, perhaps:
sportsmanship, reserve, who knows.

Somehow appropriate though:
dressed in white, competitive -
but so well mannered.

It fits the myth:
the benevolent overlords -
something to declare; impossible targets.

I've been at silly-point, all my life -
dropping balls, missing the wicket.

I remember at school,
the captain picking the team:
me twelfth-man as usual -
beyond all boundaries.

I'd like to have been up front, of course:
the fine-cut, the hook -
ripples of applause.

Still, never mind ol' chap:
stiff upper lip -
there's always, the follow-on.

BYPASSED

If I want to get into town,
I have **Three** choices:

One: the aerial route -
a series of slopes and concrete-bridges,
designed for the Sherpa and a string of mules.

Two: the subterranean -
tunnels of graffiti and mosaic,
home to the skate-board and prospective muggers.

Three: the roundabout -
a labyrinth, whose entrances and exits,
defy the convolutions of the brain.

If I want to get into town,
I have **Three;** choices?

BLACK COFFEE

When I can't sleep,
I go to the early morning cafe.

The same people eat there -
day-in, day-out.

The punter, who talks form:
who always loses -
but only just.

The workman, with his paper:
cloth-cap and dungarees -
hands, ingrained.

I listen to the banter:
the daily news dissected -
comments and opinions.

When anyone comes in, it's.......

"'ave you read this, it's all bloody wrong,
I fink; should never be allowed."

Or........

"There you are, what did I tell yer,
it was bound to 'appen."

They don't miss a thing:
race, sex, religion -
you name it, they'll discuss it.

The owner's name is Ali:
Ali Baba, they call him -
make jokes about black-looks; suntan.

"Oi you, char-wallah, where's my bacon sarnie -
you bin on bleedin' safari, or what?

Ali, manipulates the'Stills' -
lets-off; steam.......

'SMALL BOATS' (LEIGH-ON-SEA - ESSEX)

We drove to the marshes on Bonfire-Night:
it was an odd experience -
horizon to horizon, peppered with star-bursts -

light and colour
climbing through darkness
and the air's percussion.

I could hear the waders
and the slow, oncoming tide -
whistles and whispers over flats and saltings.

A firework - of some down-floating kind -
hung flare-like in the haze above the creek.
The cockle-boats were ghosted on my mind -
each silhouette, a glimmering of France.

CRYSTAL GAZING

Where am I going in the snow?
here, at my tracks' end,
hoping for something
that I cannot name.

I remember, as a child,
following the same light -
guile-less on a winter's road
leading from nowhere
into veils of silence.

Where am I going in the snow?
the tracks behind me
close to their meanings
in a wake of whispers:

the air, as soundless,
as the cold is dense -
flakes into fragments
of unmatched perfection.

"NICE WEATHER WE'RE HAVING"

This year,
I got a thermometer for Christmas -
one of the maximum and minimum variety.

As far as the jargon goes,
it's both hot, and cool -
is de rigueur for the amateur meteorologist.

How many neighbours have you got
who could give you the daily range
in both centigrade and Fahrenheit?

Strangely - it seems to me -
they're not impressed -
can't see the point of it all.

Nevertheless - at 09.00. GMT - I'm there,
clipboard at the ready, pencil licked.

Conscientiously, I record the data -
make notes on anything exceptional
and calculate the monthly averages.

Indoors - figures at hand -
I check against previous entries -
look for anomalies, correspondences.

After breakfast, I pick up the paper -
turn to the weather-maps
and assess the predictions.

Having re-set the barometer
and tapped it several times,
    I go back to bed.

I could go out - according to the graph
the temperature is way above its mean -
but what's the point, if meeting, even friends,
one finds oneself, with nothing, left to say?

PIGEON-POST

When in the queue at the post-office
I pass the time by looking through the leaflets.

This week, a language pamphlet, caught my eye:
'A foreign tongue in three months,' it claimed,
'Start now, amaze yourself, your friends, your family.'

Gobbledygook, more like, I thought,
even double-dutch is difficult.

When I got to the counter
I asked for a passport application form
and duly received - in triplicate -
a look that only postal clerks are famed for.

At home - in need of an EEC. directive -
I attempted the impossible,
'bureaucracy in twenty minutes'.

I having failed at the first three questions
I stood on my head and repeated the word:
'officialese' ten thousand times.

On righting myself - in terms of both
     gravity and composure -
I walked across to the window, opened it,
and retrieved a pigeon from the ledge.

To this, I attached a four page letter, in Esperanto,
affixed a first-class stamp to its sconce,
and hurled it - lick-lick-monkey - into space.

SUMMER DEEP

Rain in the afternoon -
The diffuse light gathers its beads on the window
And the world outside wavers into glooms of greenness.

I am deep beneath these melancholic waters:
Subaqueous in solitude -
Plankton in the mind's uncharted ocean.

A blackbird adds to sadness with its song
And slowly, down the thermocline of sound,
Each liquid note diminishes to silence.

This room, becomes a capsule,
Where life is gauged through books and faded prints -
The clock ticks out its threnody of time
And something gives, is buckled, under pressure.

RED HERRING

In those days we caught the 3.50 to Fenchurch Street:
the porter's special, they called it -
full-steam for Billingsgate.

Men from Shoeburyness and Leigh on Sea
trawled-up in the luggage-racks -
their snores as loud as waves against the beach.

What were they dreaming of in that art-deco
world of railway-posters -
the Flying-Scot traversing in their sleep
some bridge between the mountains and the isles?

And what of me, somnambulant, sixteen,
swaying to the rhythms of the track -
the smell of fish, the herring-fleet at sea,
tobacco-smoke, as tangy, as a cure.

MAY DAY

Too slight to drown; too weak to fly away,
A moth or some-such thing without renown
Just struggles with the water's surface tension.

It's May, and the river's perfect calm
Repeats the day through each inverted image.

A field of rape is swallowed by a wood
And. the sky is crazed by cirrus under blue.

A cuckoo - in its repetitious way -
Intrudes across the distance and the haze;

Too slight to drown, too weak to fly away,
A moth or some-such thing without renown
Diffuses into circles; into waves.

A LARK IN SUMMER

When you think of England, you think of the vicarage:
you think of the vicar and his shelves of books -
Wisden on one side, Donne on the other.

Here, between two large towns, set square
within its own green acres;
Sutton-with-Shopland
relives the dream of England and its shires.

Screened from the road by an avenue of limes,
this poem of a bygone age, rhymes through the summer
with its Georgian metric. Apple and pear,

primed by the blackbird and the evening thrush -
glare in the sunset, like a line of music.
Vaughan Williams, is walking with the squire,

between the hoops, haphazard on the lawn,
    and Meredith, a moment in their minds,
        is borne aloft, to shine on lyric wings.

CLODS

Recently, I was given the name; 'clay-kicker',
not as an insult, you understand,
    nor taken as such.

    If as a child
you'd walked the Essex fields,
you'd know exactly, what was meant.

I can still remember the weight:
the clodded feet,
grown to enormous size -
impediment to every step.

I thought I was a giant:
fee-fo-fumming in the wind -
showered with autumn from exploding elms.

When it got too heavy
you gave a kick and away it flew,
great glutinous lumps spattering the furrows.

All in vain though, a few more steps
and you were back where you started -
a diminutive clod-'opper,
wearing the weather, like your father's shoes.

END OF SEASON

Summer ends on days like this -
as if looking the other way
you miss the steps
the weather means to take.

Hard to say when, exactly:
the showman's voice
less poignant than before -
no pressing need
for trips around the bay.

The tide far out from
light's forgotten shore,
where littorals are silts
of solemn grey
and gulls no more
than stilted in reflections.

The kiss-me-quick
is now as good as done -
excepting where the sun's
undaunted rays eclipses thought
and splays between the clouds.

ARDROSSAN TO BRODICK

Slowly the Islands draw us into view -
Arran, with Goat-Fell, looming in the clouds,
Assumes the role that's loftily its own.

Cumbrae and the Holy-Isle
Play out alone, their separate minor parts,
Where weather is the style and the pose
That traps them in the limelight of the sun.

Across the white sheer-water of the waves
The ferry with its gallery of gulls -
overcomes the pull of mainland art
And plunges to the harbour's final act.

CIRCUS

I like the man on stilts:
his jester's outfit -
the silly tricks for children.

I'm built for such things:
the motley and the bells -
the irreverent hooter.

The way he holds out his hand,
pretending as if to shake,
then thumbing his nose.

It makes me laugh:.
simple I suppose -
predictable.

People say I'm daft
for liking such things;
perhaps they're right.

I've tried to be more serious:
to study the slick magicians -
the illusionists.

Not for me I'm afraid:
slapstick's more my mark -
the custard-pie; the banana-skin.

Sometimes it hurts,
even innocence
has its drawbacks.

But it's really not so bad,
there's always the funny walk,
the painted smile; teardrops.

FIRST IMPRESSIONS

As a child I followed her everywhere -
I remember the seams of her stockings
and where they went.

She had a fifties figure:
a jacket tightly cut -
all curves and a pencil skirt.

I was mesmerized by the sway of hips -
the swell of her breasts.

Love-struck, as I was,
I kept a respectful distance -
kept my crush at a remove.

Although embarrassed by the sport
she took it in good part -
added a wiggle for encouragement.

When I look at women nowadays
I find that she's superimposed -
that I've followed her all my life.

AUTUMN FORECAST

Plumes of cirrus
bury their fibres
in the lactic-blue;

like a sprawling thallus
threading its hyphae
through the sky's rich humus.

Iridescent rings
fruit in profusion
round the fungal orb;

and the light's thin soil
darkens with dankness
into spores of rain.

THROUGH A GLASS BRIGHTLY

I used to hold my hand
against the frozen window
until it burnt with the cold
and cleared a patch just
large enough to see through.

In the starlit hours
gold from the downstairs rooms
overlay the snow on the lawn
and flowers of frost
ghosted from the winter rose-bush.

Those were the silent nights
that held me spellbound -
clouds like glittering Magi
sailed out across the moon
towards Epiphany.

At St Joseph's seminary
I'd been told what holiness was
but compared with this
religion was frigid -
ice without the sparkle.

ALL SAINTS

Today the organ repairers were at work
and snatches of hymns encouraged us to enter.

The church that is normally closed, even
on Sunday afternoons, greeted our eyes
with its pure, whitewashed simplicity.

Sunlight through stained-glass
streamed over seasonal flowers
raising their colours to a religious pitch.

I genuflected automatically to the discordant
strains of 'Onward Christian Soldiers'
and circuits long bypassed were suddenly reconnected.

The unlikely trinity tinkered deeply with
    sound's arcane mechanics
and their occult whisperings surfaced like oblations.

SOUTH DOWNS

Berries, leaves and light
are autumn's heraldry -
nature's succession.

Noblesse oblige finds beeches
lording it over the downs -
emblazoned in hangers.

Hawthorn and brier
are heir to the season -
wear traveller's joy; like ermine.

EASTBOURNE PIER

The starlings swirl like smoke
in the sun's last embers.

The air is choked with sound
as they settle on the girders of the pier.

Wary of the slightest noise
they shake the cloak of themselves
back into the evening sky;

turn as one, swerve
and follow the same invisible track
down to the place where they started.

Like crickets in the summer grass
their voices rise and fall or pause in unison.

Through the planking of the pier
I can see the fluttering mass
as they jostle for position in the roost.

I stamp my foot -childishly -
and a thousand threads of black
fray out across the whiteness of the surf.

HANNINGFIELD RESERVOIR

Above the causeway
the swifts congregate.

As sure as the psalms
the evening hatch is there.

Thousands of wings
scythe through the
   darkening air -
reap the rewards of faith.

MISNOMER

Whatever happened to flaming June -
this year's misnomer.
The roses bloom the same
but their petals fall on the slanted wind
like a rain of perpetual butterflies.
Birds hunch-up their feathers
dishevelled and dripping from branches
as the clouds unload their continuous freight.

This is no time for the north -
for Boreas and his frigid breath.
 It should be sun and sandwiches,
        bees and blossom.
But death is the small pink flesh
spewed from the fledging gutters
and life but a few stray poppies
bleeding through ragwort and a broken fence.

CHURCH-END PAGELSHAM

The robinia flowers in the churchyard
and the copper beech offers a contrast..

Pollarded limes sprout with leaves
and a greenfinch sings from a headstone.

In the distance we hear the thwack
of leather on willow,
followed by a ripple of applause.

On the porch door there's a notice:
'please keep closed, swallows trying to nest'.

We soak in the sun and the sanctity -
bless the hearts carved on an ancient bole.

MERIDIAN

I listen to the
willow warbler
and summer seems
almost tangible.

Its cadences drift
over the meadow
and fade in the listless heat.

Comfrey and mallow
glaze in the noon glare -
blur into mauves and purples.

Swallows and terns
follow the grain of the river -
touch at a tangent.

SONG AT DUSK

The blackbird sings at dusk
and I could almost trust in God.

Things seem infinitely possible
as it flutes at the new moon.

In that hush before the stars
it pitches notes into the darkness.

Soon it will all be silence
but for now the spheres are singing.

WOODHAM FERRERS

The fields are bleached by sunlight
and the evening slows to hay on loaded trailers.

Trees cast long shadows and a bunting
from the telegraph jangles its bunch of keys.

A church on the skyline catches the slant
of the sun - is touched by Midas.

PASSING SUMMER

In those days it was different:
I chose to be full of life -
to notice the world about me.

It was easy to see God
at work in the veins of a leaf -
in the song of a blackbird.

But now I begin to believe
there's no going back -
no recapturing the past.

I hear the children
laughing in the street
and try to remember
the days before grief took over.

Hogweed and mallow
tower over waste land:
their flowering a sort of sadness -
a ghostly collusion.

Look as hard as I might
the butterfly's wings are frail -
their span ephemeral.

BRIDAL

New year's day
and a fall of snow:
not much, but enough
to whiten the roads -
to slow the traffic.

We crawl into town
over a grid of tyre tracks.

Flakes as large as wild roses
scatter in our wake,
then flutter to the ground.

People are hunched
against the north:
muffled in scarves and gloves -
feeling the brunt of the weather.

New replaces old,
where like a virgin
in her wedding dress
the garment of increasing cold
lowers its veil of secrecy and silence.

GARGOYLES

They say it's the land of witches
and I must admit to a twitch

when hereabouts. Look at the church,
imagine if you can a birch-

broom flying across the tower,
the hands at the midnight hour

and the full moon struck in the sky.
In this modern age we rely

on science for our share of truth.
Hobgoblins and such need the proof

of our own eyes. I see them here,
albeit without the mind's clear

wisdom. Carved in the Kentish stone
I find the resurrected bones

of an older way of seeing -
a devilish philosophy.

MOON

I'm watching the man in the moon, left to himself
I think he could croon a deep, bass song.

The clouds throng around, but he's
soundless, and one by one they shuffle off.

Now he's alone I'm sure that he'll clear his throat and sing,
but no, the wing of a bird tickles his silver nose -

       perhaps he'll sneeze instead.
I go to my bed disappointed - music has been eclipsed.

SUBURBIA

Eve's now middle aged
but her garden's still paradisal.

She wages war against the weeds,
plants fuchsias and geraniums.

When the weather's fine
there's not a fig-leaf in sight.

Naked as God intended
she basks in her innocence.

Prone in the bronzing sun
she longs for her ancient lover.

But he as a penance for his sin -
must continue to mow the lawn.

REFLECTIONS

What was it about that evening:
the replications of the river -
the moon in duplicate?

Was it the harvest fields
sheened with a golden pallor -
the dusky trees?

For me it was your presence -
more than the yellowhammer
wheezing its summer song,
or the gregarious swallows
meeting themselves in our mirror.

TRANSPORTED

The swifts are gone and the long
summer nights are nearly over.

The barbecue glows in the dark
and the moon is as red as the rising sun.

People are chatting in small groups
and the bats are hawking moths.

A cricket rubs its legs in the distance
and place: is no longer - England.

AUTUMN WOODS

Gossamers are slung, branch to branch -
live-wired, by the misted sunlight.

The static of the loosened leaves
   patters through silence.

   Squirrels flow with ease -
complete their lissome circuitry.

Acorns fall from their sockets -
   thud to earth.

Bulbs of fungi glow red and mauve -
   are in their element.

GUY FAWKES

Our guy was short on sartorial elegance -
the average scarecrow was better dressed.

Clothes from the rag-bag,
scrunched-up newspaper,
bits of string and a mask.

We were proud of it though -
carted the thing all round town
on a clapped-out trolley.

We propped it up by the post-box
and were ready for business.

'Penny for the guy mister'
when secretly we were hoping
for thruppenny-bits and tanners.

I got a shilling once -
more than a whole week's pocket-money.

It was the epitome of autumn:
elms like roman-candles in the mist -
leaves cascading.

Our thoughts were like jumping-crackers -
exploding from one thing to another.

Bonfires and rockets,
baked spuds and squibs.

Only the rain could dampen our enthusiasm:
but for now the fog moved in -
the street lamps - like Catherine-wheels.

AUTUMN BLACKBIRDS

The lawn is wet with dew -
crystals on the edge of frost.

A blackbird turns its head
and plucks a worm.

It flirts its tail
runs a few feet
then stops;

turns its head again
and starts the procedure all over.

Another under the hedge
scratches in dry leaves -
chooses a different larder.

Its autumn song
is stilled to the ring of glass -
a repetitive chink.

The garden is ready for winter:
trees are bare, windfalls fermenting.

The air is chill with the thoughts of snow to come -
the blackbird's beak - as yellow as a crocus.

1996-2000

NOAH'S WIFE

She lived in a houseboat on the creek -
a frail old lady as weak as the willowy reeds.

Winter or summer she wore
wellingtons and a mackintosh -
was witness to the shelduck and the geese.

Pushing a pram to market
she was followed by her tribe of dogs -
mongrels with a touch of mange.

She had an arrangement with the butcher -
bought lights and was given bones
to feed her whining multitude.

Children giggled in her wake:
were rude to the point of cruelty -
taunting and merciless.

Back on her boat she was at peace:
soothed by the salty wind -
calmed by the call of curlews.

Water from the farm
and driftwood for her range
she had ample for her needs.

Time and tide were her friends:
the skittering, sunlit waves -
as welcome as doves - an olive branch.

AFTER FREEZING FOG

It's cold along the river
  and the quiet
is almost tangible.

Reeds are furred with frost
and slithers of thin ice
cling to the margins
with their frigid fingers.

The fish are lying deep -
  jewels in a casket.

This is winter's heraldry:
trees are armorial -
feathered fleur-de-lis.

A crow is a black prince
flying over white fields
and the ice-queen touches
  the umbellifers.

On mornings such as these
we're in the reign of light:
gold on a blue shield -
the landscape in ermine.

BRENT GEESE

Their skeins are loose
and straggling in the sky.

Like winter's drawn out signature
they fly towards the saltings.
Ten thousand exclamation marks
all ending the same sentence.

They find a paragraph of eel-grass
  and all is a full-stop.

They punctuate the mudflats
  with their puddling:

commas and semi colons -
pauses in their own biography.

Quotation marks containing the clangorous -
voices on the written wind.

FOG

The day started and ended in fog -
distances dissolved
and joggers disappeared.

The sun - a lost soul -
floated like a pale moon.

It was like living in a bowl:
trees were weeds -
birds fishes.

I needed to come up for air
but my spirit was weighted.

A bus, like a submarine
came faintly from the gloom -
splaying its yellow eyes.

SEAGULL

So self-contained
that seagull on the roof -

plays king of the castle
with his kith and kin
then stands and rules his kingdom.

What's in his mind?
He has the use of wings
yet prefers to guard his patch.

If I had his ability
would I be satisfied
with the sedentary?

In weather like this could I resist the blue -
the golden road of winter's pallid sunlight?

He twitches his feathers and is back in his element -
I preen the imperfections on the page.

ULTING CHURCH

The snowdrops are out in the churchyard
and hope surfaces amongst the granite.

A thrush is resurrected in the oak
and displays his blessed virtuosity.

January soaks in the reverential light -
leaves darkness to the devil's own disciples.

There is a stillness that's portentous -
the ghostly warmth of Easter in the bud.

Heat is reflected from devotional stone
and a cloud of gnats disseminate - like incense.

JOURNEY HOME

The snow is driven from the north -
small hard grains blown into veils of mist.

Walking home from the club,
head down against the wind,
beard caked with ice,
I come to a stop.

Limbs tired against the drifts
I stand and watch the blizzard
swirl past the street lamps -
turn the night into haloes.

This is religious weather -
all the sins of the world
are covered in a purity of whiteness.

The grass is reverential -
the frost an enlightenment of stars.

If I died, here and now,
angels could be expected -
a terminal incandescence.

Head down again
I move off into the blast:
traffic passes on holy wheels -
the bushes susurrate with prayer.

DETONATION

The garden is ready to explode:
spring sets the mechanism -
wires the clock.

Snowdrops are the fuse -
crocuses the first spark.

Daffodils wait to cannonade -
tulips hold their fire.

Half the world's in bud -
powder for the sun's ignition.

A thrush chips away at a snail
as if striking a flint -
blackbirds raise the alarm.

FIELDS OF RAPE

Rape fields are in bloom -
a yellow-scented day
framed in immaculate blue.

Swifts zoom across the flowers
with summer on their wings -
swallows loop and curve.

Bees are in their element:
up to their knees in molten gold -
droning incessantly.

We walk the lanes -
drown in the fragrance
that surrounds us.

There's no need to talk -
the colours say it all.

A pitch-black barn
shimmers with contrast
in the May heat.

Cow-parsley balances its plates
and a yellowhammer
conjures a song from the telegraph.

SPRING

The frogs have
started their chorus -
their springtime
gutturals of love.

Soon they'll be clasping
the backs of females
and the pond will
be thick with spawn.

Across the lawn
the daffodils
herald their arrival -
a yellow-throated
vibrato in the breeze.

Thrushes vie for position
with their repeated phrases
and the blackbird
is a flautist in the hedge.

Tulips are on the edge
of their summer music:
their scarlet notes -
anxious for orchestration.

DECEMBER RAIN

December rain sluices over pavements:
people tilt their umbrellas in the wind -
inch further into Advent.

Streets are garlanded with light:
windows kaleidoscopic -
crazed into many colours.

The festive trees spread out
their illuminant branches -
drip in the deluge.

At home the decorations glitter:
tinsel twirls in the heat -
coruscates with silver.

The cards hang on their strings:
bridging the gap of the year -
offering salutations.

It snows in another latitude:
images are erroneous -
belong to some other country.

The star is obscured by cloud:
shepherd's and angels
are somehow out of place -
live in the realms of history.

At midnight mass
we try to conjure the spirit
with incense and carols.

Communion doesn't work -
drunks in the congregation
spoil the bread and wine.

Nothing makes sense anymore:
the manger shrinks
from its urban setting -
harks back to the pastoral.

I pray less earnestly:
despair of the mystic past -
cry out for a new mythology.

CHRISTMAS EVE

At Christmas time
we bring the outside, inside -
make re-acquaintance with the forest.

The tree stands in the corner of the room:
festooned with lights - a welcome stranger.

Baubels and tinsel spin and glitter -
capture the spectrum.

Wooden toys dangle from the branches:
clowns and popinjays -
a Santa Claus and a rocking-horse.

The children's interest
rests with the chocolate money -
a wealth of golden memories.

Presents are stacked underneath:
wrapped in their festive colours -
named in anticipation.

Every year the same ritual -
the solstice and the new year
dressed in a Christian habit.

Outside the frost settles on the roofs of cars:
glistens on the whitening grasses -
sparkles on railings.

To-night it could all be true -
Melchior, Balthazar and Caspar
ride beneath the bright, expectant stars.

The town awaits the good news -
the roar of the traffic dies around midnight
and it's as quiet as Bethlehem.

COUNTDOWN TO MIDNIGHT

We drive into the country
and the moon flies between the trees -
hooks a reluctant cloud.

The road unfurls before us
like a roll of paper -
headlights print the news.

Cars are sparkling in the frost:
imaginary constellations -
encrusted with diamonds.

When we stop in the car park
Orion's belt greets our arrival -
dominates the sky.

The Pleiades are hard to count:
blur to a white smudge -
astonish with distance.

The bar is festooned with lights:
glasses glitter on the shelves -
bring the heavens indoors.

We wassail the season
with our friends -
pay homage's to yuletide.

The Christian overlay is thin:
corn-dollies hang from the tree -
sentiments are evergreen.

Holly glistens on the hearth:
berries imitate the embers -
burn in the darkness.

Mistletoe hangs from the ceiling:
encourages kissing -
hints at fertility.

When we leave the bar
whiteness subjugates the world -
locks everything in ice.

Three staggering drunks
stumble off into wonderment -
unintelligible Magi.

FEBRUARY BLIZZARD

The river's choked with ice:
reflections have been erased -
the mirror dulled.

A swan comes in ungainly:
feet forward, wings outstretched -
enters a private slalom.

Willows are held by the hair:
branches taut against the wind -
winter's Aeolian harps.

Snow gusts across the fields:
builds its bulk against the hedgerows -
creates an arctic sculpture.

On the lake the Canada-geese
paddle across solidity -
lose their equipoise.

The blizzard comes on again -
grains as fine as chalk-dust
eradicate the hills.

Everything closes in -
sound diminishes
and snow becomes omnipresent.

The whiteness is like a cocoon:
deep in the earth changes are taking place -
metamorphoses - impinge.

STARLING ROOST

The starlings gather at the roost -
great swirling veils
that twist and turn in unison.

As they move in and out of earshot
the whir of their wings
sounds like waves on a shingle beach.

They settle on the barn roof:
a quivering mass of feathers -
a living thatch.

A length of cloth is shaken
and they lift again as one -
a cacophony of murmurations.

Blocking out the sky
they furl and unfurl
keeping the air in purdah.

It's as if they'll never stop:
periodically they fall but to rise again -
oscillate the senses.

Slowly the activity lessens:
sporadic twitterings highlight the uncertainty -
worry the equilibrium.

Light is draining fast
and a sense of urgency
answers the instinctive question.

Collectively they come to rest:
silence is suddenly intensified -
dusk authenticated.

GANG

We were a dastardly gang of children:
bristling with armaments -
bows and arrows, catapults, air-guns.

We had a camp in a hawthorn thicket -
a makeshift command centre
where we made our battle plans.

Ambushes were a speciality -
lying in wait down the alley
for any passing stranger.

Saturday mornings were the best -
kids coming home from the flicks
loaded with sweets; money.

"Stand and deliver you varlets;
give us your valuables."

You should have seen their faces -
ready to burst into tears
as they emptied their grubby pockets.

Laden with guilt and ill-gotten loot
we headed for the hinterland -
divided up the spoils.

I'm sure there was a bounty on our heads -
a posse of parents tried to hunt us down
but couldn't follow our tracks.

We weren't afraid of the lynch-mob:
back at the camp we lit the victory fire -
feasted on bull's-eyes and mint-imperials.

TAKE-OVER

Trees come into leaf:
put on their summer dress -
rustle their skirts.

A willow-warbler tries its song
and the long drawn cadence
trickles down the drying air.

The sun sizzles at the zenith
and the sky's blue pallor
curves to the green horizons.

The river quenches its thirst for images:
inverts alder and ash -
gulps at a passing cloud.

Swallows are skimmed across the surface
and their fragile bodies
bounce back into northern latitudes.

Coots squabble in the margins:
shatter the peace with intrusive voices -
desecrate the inviolable.

A cuckoo rings its double note
and distance is located -
the hills brought closer.

There's a take-over from the south:
meadows invest in gold -
pay dividends with buttercups.

ST. PETER'S - PAGELSHAM

The church looks out across the harvest fields -
Its cold grey stone yields to the waves of wheat
And builds a solemn silence deep within.

St Peter steps out of a stained-glass boat -
Walks over to Christ and the Apostles
Who seem to float in the uncanny light.

A shipwright must have timbered such a roof:
It moves through the swell of air like a hull -
Is loosed on the tide in a buffeting wind.

The whole place founders in the flow of dusk -
Is hushed like the ribs of a fathoming wreck
That comes to rest amongst shoals of swallows.

Here in the chancel of a deep sea cave
The fabric prays for the safety of our souls
And faintly holds a whisper like a shell.

OCTOBER MIST

Today it's October mist:
The tincture of ring-doves -
Crop-full on summer.

The river is bleary-eyed:
Slurs the inverted world -
Imbibes on atmosphere.

A jay is suddenly exotic:
Shouts of a foreign land -
Is raucous with colour.

Dragonflies scan the air:
Choose an erratic metre -
Are at odds with autumn.

Spiders set out to work:
Trace sheer geometries -
Trammel the breeze.

The leaves descend in droves:
Pattern the waiting grass -
Inlay, like mosaic.

APRIL SWALLOWS

The swallows gather back about the farm
Along the self-same tracks they made last year.

I hear them twitter, careless on a curve,
Careering over waves of winter-wheat

To climb the thermal ladder rung by rung.
The early heat has summoned up their wings -

Has brought them back to swing across the breeze
And catch the hapless insects in their flight.

The glancing light reveals their backs' blue sheen
And brightens up the russet on their throats.

They seem to float quite effortless on air
As blest in pairs they race around the barn

Without their feathers offering a sound.
The warm thanksgiving weather from the west

Has found them once again on summer's edge
To revel as they roister round the fields
And pledge themselves to April's subtle skies.

HEATWAVE

The diamond light dazzles through the summer afternoon -
is almost faceted. A yellowhammer wheezes from the wires.
Takes its cue from the sun and basks in the breathless air.
Swallows follow the curve of the sky. Cut into molten glass.
Scry in the river. The fields of golden wheat are drowned
in mirages - turned into phantom lakes. Above the reeds
swarms of convolving gnats are drawn to the body's heat -
are niggling distractions. The damsel flies dowse their
blues and reds and greens -are glittering metallics. Warblers
unhinge the silences. Wind up their ratchets - worry the
ear with staccato voices. With half a sigh there comes a
summer breeze -a sudden breath that coruscates on water.

RAMSONS

The ramsons grow in clusters by the hedge
to compliment our Easter expectations.

We seem to recognise them as a pledge -
that summertime is eager to select

rare blooms instead of winter's altercations.
We've had enough of April and its showers

with dampness the demeanour of the day
and cumulus the prophecy that towers.

The weeping cherry celebrates in pink
the blatant blue of spring's contrasting skies

where petals scatter earthwards on the wind
and bless the grass with more than our surmisals.

This is the time of year we would not miss
where flowers raise their colours from their beds

and blackbirds flute and thrushes start to whistle.
There is a quiet delirium that spreads

through every sense that touches on a nerve,
as if the mind had brushed against a thistle.

The sun's as hot as tulips burning red
and swallows chase their shadows on a curve.

ADESTE FIDELES

I'm remembering a season
When tradition had its way
And the snow began to fall on Christmas-Eve;
When the midnight's holy reason
Had us kneeling down to pray
With the fervency of those who still believe.

It was not the trick of tinsel
Or the baubles on the tree
That inveigled our spontaneous response;
But imagination kindled
By a star we half perceived
In the candlelight that flickered from the sconce.

When *Adeste* and *Fideles*
Brought the service to a close
We were ready to negotiate the night;
And we left behind the baby
in its porcelain repose
To investigate the verities of white.

Like an angel's shaken feathers
Down meanderings of air
Came the muted multiplicity of flakes;
Every one of them six-sided
Individual and rare
Like epiphanies that crystallize in space.

Once indoors we left the snowfall
To its seasonal device
And ascended the quiescence of the stairs;
Where on every bedroom window
The cold artistry of ice
Had depicted how the weather said its prayers.

A MOONLESS EQUILIBRIUM

At least the weather knew its rightful place.
Seasons were seasons. Snow succeeded fog
On traditional trees and belief in God
Wondered at the wood's unsung cathedral. Faith

Blossomed in spring and flowers followed
On from frost. Leaves became the emblems
Of the year and the butterflies remembering
The sun were harbingers of swallows

On the wing. But now all seasons are as one.
Patterns settle down to rain and wind
And temperature tries hard to comprehend
Its lost extremes. The range becomes none

Other than a farce. A middling heat
That neither warms nor chills. A moonless
Mediocrity, that darkens and undoubtedly depresses -
Except where lamps wear haloes down the street.

ACQUITTAL

Every day the same:
Wind from a dubious quarter -
The obliquities of rain.

Inclemency prevails:
A crow traverses limits -
Feathers its pinions.

The standing water
Implicates the sky -
Bears witness to disorder.

Night is inculpable:
The moon between clouds -
Weathers its defense.

GARDEN PARTY

The garden waits for spring:
Mingles with the frost -
The fishpond, bleary.

Even the blackbird
Tarries with his song:
"Chink, chink, chink,"
Glass against glass -
A toast to better weather.

The sun in a low arc
Has no influence with ice -
Chatters to a blue guest.

The snowdrops start to gossip:
Their nodding heads
Acquainted with the breeze -
Intimates, partygoers.

At twelve-o-clock
The icing takes the hint -
Softens a little.

The crocuses are tinder to the eye:
Oracles that flicker with a wish -
Candles, on the cake.

GOLDEN HARVEST

In the land of never after
I explored the country ways
With a band of ragamuffins for my friends;
Where the sun as loud as laughter
Saw us hurtle through the maze
Of what now, or when, or how, and it depends.

Through the marshes wound the magic
Of a serpentine embrace
As the creeks just slithered in on scales of gold;
Where a swan as white as whispers
Was the apogee of grace
And the agent of a miracle foretold.

Over fields as far as heaven
Thick with butterflies and flowers
We'd matriculate on lessons made of light;
Where the crickets' harsh devotion
To the deity of hours
Lasted well into the homily of night.

In the somnolence of shadows
We would sit beneath the elms
Still unconscious of the potentates of time;
No attrition could divide us
From the fortress of ourselves
As we nestled in the nexus of a rhyme.

In the latter days of August
We would amble round the farms
Through a mirage made of happiness and heat;
Where the men knee-deep in poppies
Read the weather's open palms
And brought in the ghost of summer with the wheat.

MUCKING (ESSEX)

Have you ever been to Mucking
Down by Thameside in the marsh
Where the world has passed perceptibly away;
Where the isolated farmsteads
Are reminders of the past
When rotation was the rhythm of the age.

There are reeds they call phragmites
That stretch out on either hand
Into featherings of unrestricted light;
Though succession tries to turn them
Into dry un-sodden land
Conservationists are equal to the fight.

Bearded reedlings build their nests there
When the sun begins to soar
And seclusion hides the bunting and the rail;
Cuckoos pay their yearly visits
To the warbler's open door
And their eggs are unsolicited, like mail.

There's a church that's turned domestic
Now parishioners are few
And religion cedes its consecrated ground;
Time's irreverence has dated
Both the lectern and the pew
And the hymnal is a far forgotten sound.

In an acreage of silence
When September soothes like balm
And the ivy's a perversity of flowers;
Cabbage-whites and bright red-admirals
Sing the weather's muted psalms
Like a legacy of lost angelic powers.

THE IMMEMORIAL ELMS

I remember Bowers Gifford
When the countryside had elms
And the cattle browsed all summer through the marsh;
When the saws were wise on weather
And the sky was overwhelmed
By the rippling high cadenza of the lark.

Now St Margaret's looks dejected
Even though the graves are kempt
And its had the brave addition of a spire;
But there's something penitential
When the soul becomes exempt
And the spirit leaves the precincts of the choir.

There are still the turning seasons
And the rhythm of the land
That is punctuated yearly by the plough;
Many rhymes and many reasons
That we try to understand
Like the rhapsody of blackbirds on the bough.

In-between the roads and railway
Down an old forgotten lane
There is still the sun's soliloquy of gold;
Where the shadows fall obliquely
In an effort to explain
How the evening light surrenders and consoles.

As I wander into autumn
Through the sauntering of leaves
And the pheasant's quick discordancy of sound;
All my memories are haunted
By the ghosts of former trees
That have turned decomposition into ground.

REMAINDERED

I should like to stay in Terling
Now that autumn's come around
And the old-man's-beard is hoary down the lane;
Where the silver skies are sterling
With the hallmark of the clouds
And the story's cold denouement turns to rain.

Where the narrative of summer
Has developed into gold
And the written earth is redolent of musk;
Where each paragraph and chapter
Has a plot it must resolve
Like the hazel-nut concluded in the husk.

From the shelter of the covers
There's the whir of sudden wings
As each partridge turns its phrase into a clause;
Over fields of feint and margin
As if arrows loosed from strings
They eschew the modulation of a pause.

By the ford the fluent waters
Make a copy of the sky
That is punctuated nightly by the rooks;
Where the light's amanuensis
Takes dictation with a sigh
And the shaken leaves illuminate a book.

High above the church arid steeple
There's a newly published moon
That is read by the romantically inclined;
Though the day has been remaindered
I'm still privileged to choose
From the limited editions of the mind.

I.M. ELIZZA GOZZET

(A child accidentally burnt to death in the 19th century)

I have travelled down to Ulting
Every season of the year
With the temperament of autumn on my mind;
Where Eliza Gozzet's headstone
Has an epitaph that sears
Like a burning thought that time has underlined.

Such a place beside the river
For the memory of a child
Who accurses Heraclitus and his fire;
But sometimes on Sunday mornings
We remember that she smiled
And a phoenix takes possession of the choir.

She is there to watch the barges
As the horses draw their loads
Through a century of unremitting change;
Where the waterways would argue
With the railway and the road
As to who had the capacity and range.

As November mist is haunted
By the fathoming of leaves
That have emphasized detachment on the air;
There's an insubstantial something
That has brought me to my knees
As remembrance turns the moment into prayer.

She is there beside the alders
In a pinafore and smock
Throwing pebbles one by one into the flow;
And the radiating waters
Like the movement in a clock
Calculate as much of hours as we know.

AUTUMN MANUSCRIPT

At All-Saints beside the Chelmer
There's a reverential glare
That illuminates the seasonal demise;
Where transitional recorders
Are as legible as prayer
And the trees wear autumn vestments as a guise.

On the river's swirling parchment
A calligraphy of leaves
Has been gilded by the impress of the sun;
In the sky a faint disorder
Is a scrawling line of geese
Who have flighted as the ink begins to run.

In the context of the weather
There are paragraphs of light
That dispel the solemn litany of rain;
Incunabula, together
With the manuscripts of sight
Show the urgent need to worship and explain.

Out across the water-meadows
As all histories condense
There's the chilling obfuscation of the mist;
Where the quill outlives the feather
In the ordering of tense
And the runes of partiality persist.

Like a medieval rubric
Or the imprint of a seal
The distended sun steals silently away;
Is the landscape as it's written
One apocryphal or real -
Are the furrows still indicative of clay?

2001-2006

ANONYMOUS

The sun is newly minted. A gold coin
Rubbed in a blue palm. The crocuses are
Paper-money; stashed in a grass bank. Cans
Of beer, blossom by a park-bench. In clothes
A scarecrow wouldn't call his own, a man

Imbibes on spring. His thoughts are not on Lent;
He's given-up much already. Along
The borders, daffodils decide to spend
Their wealth; mock his predicament. Pigeons
Croon in circles. No thought of pounds or pence

Alters the weather's dowry. Light's soft glaze
Filters through the leafless trees. Drunkenness
Has taken its effect. He makes his way
Unsteadily - pocketed but penniless -
With March and all its flowers, just a haze.

LOST

The woods are dead. Above - the branches etch
A cloudy sky. Below - the mould is mixed
With winter rain. Each root is like a ketch

Beneath its mast - where tattered sails are shaken
By the wind and single leaves are pennants
In the blast. A squirrel leaves its wake

Among the twigs - as like a wave it wends
Across the air - then comes to rest. We take
Our bearings deep within the glade and send

Our subtle morse between the trees. A sketch
Is all we ask - a mental chart - a fix.
We need to save our souls beneath this fetch -

Where drowning thoughts are sifted through the brake
And aspiration - crippled by the bends.

CHEMOTHERAPY

The chemo and the autumn go together:
A season when the cells are in decline -
A dying time for in or outer weather.

A cocktail like the colours of the leaves
   that fade and fall:
The mind's as hoar as frost - each
   thought is targeted.

The robin's song is melancholy's ghost -
   a misted wraith.
Winter is the only place to go -

Where all the stark anatomies impose
And trace their bifurcations on the sky.
   Snow lays down its purity:

A cerement where the snowdrop speaks of hope -
   a landscape cleansed.
   The sap will rise again -
A blood renewed; that infiltrates

The crocus and the squill - and bathes in light.
Autumn was the illness in our lives
But in the veins: there's therapy - and spring.

GREEN WOODPECKER

The ocean-swell of bluebells in the woods
Compels me in my passage out of town
To navigate by stitchwort - as I should.

The sun is in the crow's-nest of a crown
Where leaves assess the light in golden waves
And mime the seas. The campion won't drown

In spring's full-tide, where sunlight gently laves
The shadowed ground and surges to the limits
Of the trees. A subaquatic cave

Gives up its ghost: no albatross this swimmer
Through the shades, who boasts the weather's trick
On wings of green and names himself

The popinjay of laughter. White-horses kick
The hawthorn into blue - and flood the skies.
Across the landlocked meadows - double quick -

The cuckoo's southern shanty lifts and dies
And leaves the lubber's heart a deep surprise.

SOUTHCHURCH HALL

Sometimes in spring there comes a perfect day:
Exactly what it is, I couldn't say

For sure. Something to do with the geese, as white
As the sky is blue. Perhaps the rudd, bright

And golden in the pond's rich ore, complete
The sense of treasure in the mind. The heat

Is like July: the sycamore, a cage,
Where freedom is both possible and gauged

By every silver note the blackbird sings.
The swifts are back on semi-precious wings -

Inlaid - like jet - in May's unfathomed air,
To please the eye. Everything's as rare

As gilded light, where amethyst can
Turn the lilac's head and fragrance span

The emptiness of space. The weeping-willows
Have no time for tears; nor tales of woe -

Their grace is that of emerald that fans
And parts the fearless breezes as they blow.

LONG-TAILED TITS

Twenty-two at the last count -
One brood? Unlikely.
Then why in mid-July
Do they flit about
With winter on their minds?

The question undulates:
I'm inclined to think
The calculus sublime -
How many angels dance
On the heads of pins?

They make a feathered
    marquetry of sky -
Dark against blue ground.
Once more I ask for answers -
They - in their turn - reply.

Their twitterings enumerate
    on air -
An abacus of light.
Why are their sums so relevant?
Why are the words so rare?

THE GREEN MAN

Spring has a feeling all his own. A touch
That brings the south into the land and leaves
The skin to tingle in the sun. A thief
Of light who's spendthrift with his gains and blushes
With the bullfinch in the thorn. Someone just
Large on life. A man of green who breezes
Through the trees and charges every leaf
To show its might. His battle-cry's the thrush,

Who doubles up his April call to arms
And leaves no-one in doubt about the fight.
Swallows muster. Blooms are marshalled. The farms
Are ready for the fray: and at a height
The cumuli contend with loud alarms,
As cuckoos give the enemy a fright.

HARMONIC

The willow-warbler sings today. Such notes
That stray sublimely from the copse and touch
The blackthorn's symphony of white. A ghost

Of tones; recorded like the thrush's clutch
Of eggs, that ring with all the colours
Of the sky and bring to earth as much

As light allows. I contemplate the flowers.
Celandine in yellow chords. The stitchwort
With the resonance of stars, and arbours

Where camellias surprise; rehearsing
What the summer will compose when every eye
Sees music on the stave. Another verse

Is all that I require, where blackbirds try
The tenderness of air and hear abroad
Antiphonal replies. The breezes sigh,

And April's passacaglias of cloud
Elaborate on harmonies of height
And turn the shafts of sunlight into sound.

ATMOSPHERIC

A histrionic place. A lime-lit church
Beside the river: where reflections make
A drama of the sky, and ducks and drakes
Strut out across the glass. The day's all light.
A scintillated show that's unrehearsed
Where mirages lie molten in the fields.
The backcloth's atmospheric; where sight
Ascends the gentleness of hills, that yield

A gentler view. A bluishness. A haze.
A living scene the sun cannot construe
As other than the plot. The denouement
Of humidity is rain. The thermals
Play their part. Lift up the air and paraphrase
Its lines. Condensation corpses at the tops;
Where clouds are left remembering their words
That fall to earth, declaiming, drop by drop.

MONUMENTAL

April builds its clouds. A masonry that
Towers into blue and glaciates
The mansions of the mind. Each base as black
As basalt, scarcely moves, as hail escapes

To rattle on the path. The architect
Of sunlight is confused, when showers break
And shafts of gold combine to raise a spectral
Arch across the sky. In winter's wake

The periwinkles bloom. Frail structures out
Of emptiness devised to here assume
The monuments of spring. There is no doubt
The weather will collude with those who choose

To glorify design and hear the thrush
Conclusive of such things. April builds its clouds.
The sun is dimmed. The heaven's almost hushed.
And brick by brick the skylark lays its sounds.

METAMORPHOSES

We camped beside the river. The ring-doves
Linked their syllables of sound and summer

Drowsed in heat. We fished with wheat and hemp
And tried with all our callow skill to tempt

The silver seams. The river spun its glass
With every breeze. A glancing light that passed

From wave to wave and left us in a trance
We half believed. The damsel-flies, enhanced

The balmy air. Their glint metallic wings,
Diaphanous as dreams. Our pleasure hinged

On goose-quills tipped with paint. Each subtle dip
Would flex the waiting hand and lock its grip

On subaquatic treasure. At dusk the moon
Would rise behind the ash, a gold doubloon

Suspended in the calm, as herons crashed
Ungainly to their roost. The stars were cash

In heavens open purse and pipistrelles
Converged on tracks of sound, to ring the knell

Of many hapless moths. The 'Tilley-Lamps'
Were lit, and in the grass the dews of damp

Condensed. The tawny owls conversed. Two ghosts
That rose to our deluded ears and closed

The final chapter of the day. We went
To makeshift beds - cocooned within the tent -

Where every silken syllable of light
Dissolved before our metamorphic eyes.

MARCH SNOW

The snow came overnight,
Not too thick,
Just enough to delight the senses.

The robin and the wren
Were not so sure,
Their store was poverty -
Bacon-rind and stale-bread,
The weather's blind
Solidity of water.

The holly glazed its reds -
A psalter to the blue-begotten skies
That fed the mind with passion and with praise.

What holy days are these -
When trees are draped in ermine, and the sun
Has quickened to an alchemy of gold?

A word is being said:
The crocus knows
The utterance of old -
As does the bee,
The primrose and the lark.

A memory surpassing all we know
Has told the earth that spring's remembered
    tread
Will saunter on despite the depth of cold
And kick its frozen shoes against the steps.

SHELTER

Parks and gardens are the only places
Where his sanity exists. As for the rest
There's not a lot to say. Except to trace
The ring-road on its way, between the blocks
Of concrete where the sun still comes to bless
The sanctity of glass. He walks the bridge
That arches into town and counts the cost.
He's lost a mattress, clock; a TV and fridge

To wear and tear. So now it's to the shops
To stare at all the goods he can't afford.
The rain slopes down incessantly in drops
That ricochet relentless off the paths.
The lights invite him in, but the billboards
Keep him out. They tantalize with cows
In fields of grass, or worse than that, those cars
That gobble up the country miles. What now?

He passes through the precinct with a stride
That takes him to a shelter and a bench
Where crocuses and daffodils reside.
And there he sits. His pipe alight. The smoke
Convolving upwards in a cloud that mentions
Summer dawns and wraiths of mist. So there alone
He dreams his hopeless dreams. The trees are soaked.
And one: determined bee - begins to drone.

A BEE IN OCTOBER

Late October - and a bee still works for
A living: he looks to the pansies
And the cyclamen - for him the law

Is sweetness and the sun. There is no time
In his mind - the moment is nectar
And the gift of pollen. Is this sublime?

He doesn't know. What is perfection?
He doesn't care. Look as you will - this rhyme
Is not the answer: what is reflection -

But a thought - and thoughts - you know - close doors.
Go to the flower - become - as though the bee.
Hover - in October - want no more -

Where colour is the fragrance of design
And every soul's proboscis: makes connection.

THE ROBIN AND THE WREN

They're always here -
The robin and the wren.

Childhood personified:
Emblems of a meaning

That's their own -
Christmas-cards and

Farthings on the wing.
Winter - their domain:

Huddled in boxes
To escape the frost -

Or else a flame that
Melts the fallen snow.

Size - is their secret:
Smaller than the world

We think we know -
Epiphanies and reasons

Cloaked in being.
Love and sacrifice:

Jesus and St Steven
In the heart -

Birth and death
Their seasonal reminder.

WEEPING CHERRY

The weeping-cherry sheds the pinkest tears:
Where daffodils that tarnish - as if seared -

Hang down their heads - burnt umber - turned to rust
And hear no more the blackbirds and the thrushes.

So many are the years I've watched this scene:
Where sunlight summons such a rush of green -

And love appears. The hoverfly just hums
In empty air - just audible - a mumble

In the ear - reminding me of your
Unspoken voice - that softly crooned before

The turtle-doves returned to warm the passions
We revered. We knew the hush that fashioned

Our response - where silence touched as tender
As our lips - and blossom fell. Remember

Love - such memories are dear: I cannot tell
The way you're feeling now - I'm overwhelmed

By light and all that's lush - a sense of fear.
You're near me now in body - such is clear:

But is your heart still budding - like the rose -
Or will - the weeping-cherry - shed more tears?

SNARE

Come - said the spider -
My web reflects the sun

And you are one who's
Hungry for the light.

This - you know - is autumn:
When else would silk

Be spangled by the dew?
My snare is awesome.

My threads are tenuous:
Silence is the

Gossamer that sways
And whispers its

Conclusions on the breeze.
Leaves - I capture:

They cling to me for
Comfort - believe in my

Geometry of wonder.
At night I mix the

Silvers of the moon:
You too - can be transfixed

If you desire -
Attune yourself to

My vibrating strings -
Hear love's - lost music.

LEAVES

And so they fall:
One - and then another -

A steady train
That dwindles
Down the air

And makes a pall -
A red and gold mosaic.

I do not care:
The summer may not come -
So what!

It is enough to see
The tarnished sun:

The colours spun
From autumn - to the earth -
The bright despair.

And so they fall:
One - and then another -

A glittering
On verticals
That glare

And make of all:
A mystery - a wonder.

DRYADS

When I'm in the woods
I feel different:

The breezes speak to me -
Whispers - perhaps -

But nonetheless a language.
I still believe in dryads:

Childhood pictures
Of trees with faces

Seem more than mythical -
Spirits - entities.

It's not in the mind:
Known by the grain

Of the heart -
Xylem and phloem

Of an inner feeling.
Squirrels are their messengers:

Sprites In the leaf-light
Of a dim reflection -

Grey and condensing
Like the breath on glass.

THE LIGHT BEYOND

Languish if you must -
The light still beckons.

The thrush must sing his song:
His liquid notes that

Double - and delight -
Are never wrong.

The daffodil still reckons:
Counts the yellow

Moments of the year -
Where bees in throngs

Decipher as they delve -
Transmit the code.

Count not in seconds:
Time is like the

Blossom on the pear -
A purity diminished

At a breath.
Only the sun is fecund -

And even he
Is powerless at night.

SEMBLANCE

You've seen the river before - looked in the glass
For signs - portents. What is it that you see?
Clouds - blue sky - a semblance. What comes to pass

When idling with reflections? A swallow
Divides itself: fish - swim into the sun.
Are such inversions real - can we follow

Our shape at depth - understand the mind that plumbs -
The thought that fathoms? Keep to the shallows -
Surfaces glitter. You cannot overcome

Your fears - they're deep - too deep when all you ask
Is light and air. Visions of eternity -
Another self - something behind the mask?

Don't think - the mirror shatters with a stone -
The widening rings: are golden - glint as hallows.

TRAVELLERS

Believe me - I'll tell you straight - there's more to
This than materialism. The sun -
When searched - is a matter of gas - you

Know - hydrogen and helium. Look again
At the particles - they're also made of parts.
Smaller and smaller - try to explain

Them as they disappear - where's the heart
Of a wave - of energy? I could claim
For that force - intelligence - a martyred

Thought - hanging from a cross. Just construe
The way you will - but I've seen God - have numbered
More than angels on a pin - and that's the truth.

This daffodil - perfected - in the rain
Has travelled here from realms beyond the stars.

FICTION (For Wallace Stevens)

So what if it's meaningless - why worry?
Listen to the thrush - his song should be enough
To set you free. Try not to hurry -

Sit back - savour the moment. Now is all
There is - the candles on the chestnut won't
Burn down - all time is stilled. Forget the pall -

The past is dead - the future can't be spent -
What there is - there is - so make your story tall.
It takes too long to write your life's lament -

The fiction should enthrall - should leave you happy.
Tell everyone eternity is love -
The rose endures - forget the solemn poppy.

As I write this the atoms flare and fall
From one small star - in one - small firmament.

JOHN BARLEYCORN

The fallen pears - ferment: the alcohol
Of autumn dulls the wasp - and starlings
Stagger sideways: full - content. The wholesomeness

Of summer fills the hedge - where hips and haws
Are claret to the birds and hops are golden
Goblets - not a pledge. I'm tipsy with the laws

Of sloes and gin where drunken tales are told
By every dove and draughts of wine are stored
Within the grape. This blood - emboldens:

Gives courage to confront the very soul
That summer cloaked in sugars - yeast - and barley.
In veritas - this *vino* - finds the goal -

Where light's intoxication writes the score
That fills the ears of Bacchus: and the glass.

HONEY (For Rupert Brooke)

There are bees on the umbels of the hogweed:
Honey on a plate - and the summer's clock
Stilled before ten to three. Do you agree

On the smell - dust - heat - umbellifers?
Unforgettable to me - so many
Summers gleaned from the fields of time. Earth

Has its foreign fields - but fumitory
Smokes in the purple mind and slowly burns
The pyres - made of home. In memory

Those unforgotten words: The elm trees
And the river and the sun - where time has stopped
With mallow - as it mourns: and summer breathes.

The swallows undersign the sky's blue verse
And something moves - like music: empathy.

MUTE SWANS

The marshes were my home - the creek's eternal
Silver - and the sun - singing of summer
And the silent swans. Leda - as yet - unheard

Of: the gods were gentle - swans had the wings
Of angels and the fleets were rich with eels
And golden rudd. Remembering such things -

Such light defined - can make me feel
The past is still alive - that summer lingers.
You'd think that - now - in honesty - was real:

The past as dead as frankincense and myrrh -
The memory as muted as a mummer.
But no - the swans of summer - still return -

Connecting past and present - though they're dumb -
With every myth - and moment: that reveals.

THE BEATITUDES OF SILENCE

Perhaps to wonder is enough - not to
Know - just be. To see would be sufficient
For the hour - if flowers were to choose

The watching eye - and offer love. To hear
The dove without another thought would surely
Be a sacrament revealed - a mute idea.

Could there not be abroad some other law
Where instinct - or some such - could just revere
And open wide perceptions sacred door.

If I look up into the thoughtless blue
And think no more of that vast firmament:
Will I belong to light's unwritten news

Where angels are as common as they're clear
To children - and the holy - and the poor?

GODS

Remember - said the sun: I am the one
That warms your frozen mind - your God - your sole
Provider of the light - save for the moon -

The comets and the stars. I - am not endless:
I have duration - subservience
To time: mine is a golden blessing

For the flowers - a brilliance - an essence
Made divine. There are other Gods - oh yes -
The invisible ones - those without tense

Whose thoughts indwell - the starling and the stone.
They are the recognition of the whole
Where I - am but the builder - of your bones.

I am a God - provisional - no less -
Like you - I wait the future - my transcendence.

BLACK-BIRD

I have heard the blackbird singing - listened
In April by the dawning sun to notes
That diminish any chance of frost. Have wished

By the blossom on the morning pear that white
Was the answer to my darkest thoughts.
How - when the leafage could repay my sight

Can the vision alter to the sum of nought
And dim the dimensions of emergent light?
Again it's the blackbird with its song unsought

Drying the dewdrops and the early mist -
Leaving me speechless in a world of ghosts.
Here on the edges that could offer bliss

I wait for the darkness of another night -
Crave for the silence - and the stars that slaughter.

SUN-STRUCK

Distances were drear. Lapwings roamed across
The misted fields and greenness disappeared
In banks of grey. Light was at a loss

And left unclear - where sky came down to earth
As damp as rain and moistened every minute
With its tears. There was a chill that curses

Could explain - as if the witch of winter
Cast a spell - denying at a breath the birth
Of spring. Unexpectedly a glint

Of slanted gold gave everything a gloss
Beneath the sun - and calmed our fears.
A warm, angelic order - free of frost -

Exhumed the dying moment from its hearse
And turned our eyes to summer - at a squint.

THE CHURCH OF LEAVES

The rooks remember spring - high in the trees
They carry sticks - bicker and banter.
The sunlight is serious - and they believe

Entirely in their god. This is a sermon
From the sun - words of light - homilies
Of warmth. What can they do? Be as the birds

Have always been- prompt for the church of leaves -
Passionate in prayer. There's nothing absurd
In their religion - kingdom and keys

Are one - instinct - the liturgy. No cant
Disturbs their worship - theirs is a pure belief.
They do not need the righteousness of ranters -

For them there is the doctrine of the earth
And only worms can bring them to their knees.

TOADSTOOLS

The toadstools have appeared:
Overnight it seems -

Strangers in the years
Untold demise. They gleam

In sunlight - white with gold
Pretensions - close to death -

Where every foetid breath
Delivers spores. The cold

Is their domain - relics
In the rites of autumn frost -

Where all that quickened -
Suddenly - is loss.

They are the bones of summer's
Putrid flesh - skeletal

With portents in the fall -
Eloquent - but wordless: like the dumb.

THE LARK ASCENDING

Il fait beau temps - or so they say in France -
The blackbird knows and by a chance

Decree - it sings its *chanson*
Purely from the heart. What's wrong

With English? Surely you agree
The language has felicity

Of sorts - a happiness - a touch
Of mystery. French has just as much -

Je ne sais quoi - they say - enough
To mention otherness - no bluff.

The blackbird knows the truth - celebrates
In tongues - rebukes - eliminates

The need for words. Messiaen
Knew this too - there's little scansion

In the thrush - far less in the wren.
But there we are - now all is French again.

We have Vaughan-Williams - of course -
His 'Lark Ascending' is a force

To reckon with. His music soars:
Resonates and hovers off the score -

Meredith in England - or the Loire -
It matters not - just feel it - *au revoir.*

ALL SAINTS (Ulting - Essex)

There is a church beside the river -
An ancient place of stone and flint - living

The lessons of an age that's passing.
Sermons are different now - the diving tern

Dips to the icon of its sacred self -
Shatters the instant with a dream that's delving.

The Gospel is the cadence of a warbler -
A wash of notes - that dally - as they daub

And leave the mind a mural made of sound.
Moorhens pierce the passion of their vows -

Where light reflects the image of a spire
And captures clouds. The alders - are a choir:

A whispered susurration of the air
Where leaves are tongues of language -

And preaching is the purpose of the sun.
The celebrant - is sentience - and summer

As thoughts of something other touch the ear
And visions are the vespers of revering.

Ecclesiastic order here divines
The depths that drown with miracles of fish:

The moment - in itself - is bread and wine -
Beyond the realms - of reverence - and wishes.

BUCKS CROSS COTTAGE

Snug in its own green acre - eased into
Angles by the weight of time. The garden
Like a dream: memories of distant views -

Childhood - or before - something passed
Genetically - who knows? Two lines of roses
To walk between - a fragrance that the heart

Remembers - a mystery that grows
The more uncanny. There's a path beneath
The trees - sunlight and shadow - throwing

The mind into misted focus. I believe
In Alice - The Mad Hatter: Toad of Toad
Hall - lives between the cranesbill and the heartsease.

I could die here - right now - follow the road
Of the blessed - here - by the keening thrush -
The mournfulness of doves. Light is my abode:

Lyonnesse or Atlantis? No need to rush -
The golden apples of Hesperides
Have yet to ripen - sweeten in the hush.

The summer clouds are building in the west -
Their blazoned heights: a miracle - a blessing.

BEETLES

What of the beetles - have they no friends?
Blue-black or glossed with green - they know their way
Through grass: through warming soil. So much depends

On attitude - forget your instincts -
Put your trust in God. They too belong:
Are creatures made of stardust - insects

Formed by spirit - and the sun. They have their songs
Of that you can be sure: a music in
The key of heaven - elytra - shielding wings

As sheer as angels. So much amends
Demeanour if you dare: if you can praise
The thing for what it is - both means and ends.

These - so-called - lesser beings know not sin -
They live their lives: for moments - not for trends.

CONNECTIONS

I know what I like - don't you? The spikes
Of loosestrife and the climbing bees - they please
Me - trigger emotion. So you don't like

Feelings - prefer to count the stamens and
The anthers - weigh the honey. I find
Things different - more dreamy: can stand

About for hours in the garden - my mind
At rest - not thinking. I cup my hands
Around a butterfly: it's not unkind -

I feel it beating - like a heart - it's quite
Remarkable. Connections come - like these -
Uncalled for - unexpected in the light.

The blackbird sings before me and behind -
Its every note - though thoughtless - understands.

SHIELD BUGS

Two shield-bugs making love - back to back
On the leaves of buddleia - oblivious
Of my voyeuristic habits. I track

Their every move - leaf-green and roseate -
Gems of a thoughtless urge turning their facets
To the cutting sun. Continuance is slow

Work - no need to hurry - caught in the passion
Of unnumbered aeons. I would like to go -
Leave them to their privacy. Fascination

Holds me back - I'm looking for the facts
Of each creation. This - is not frivolous:
Most of us are party to the act -

However God's relationships are known
These insects show - that love - is more than fashion.

BY THE RIVER

The snowdrops cloak the graves. A living pall
That January saves to show that death's
A moment in the mind. The leaves may fall

In autumn - such is true - but even now
With frost in every glade the swollen buds
Arrange themselves for spring. The topmost bough

Attracts an early thrush - who pours a flood
Of promise as he sings - and lights the hour.
Yes - even now - the winter's gelid blood

Remembers not the canker or the gall
But waits to warm the offices of breath.
A pallid light adorns the churchyard wall -

Where lichen glows as golden as the rudd
Who turned the cloudless summer into showers.

IN THE BUD

The bluebells - are a sky - that's unawares:
Daylight seeps through branches - steeped in gold -

Where all the white anemones unfold
In wafts of song. I have something to declare:

That like the cuckoo - I - in love am bold.
Without a thought of others - or their share -

I'll walk these woods where solitude repairs
And greet the sun. Here - nothing's bought or sold:

The yaffle's mocking laughter finds no ear
Where sound and silence - both the same - are free

And I can sense the wealth in every leaf
As light unfurls. The winter's spent - the year

Moves on anew. There is no point in grief:
The message is as warm as it is clear

Where campion and stitchwort - just appear -
Like something on the borders of belief:

Outside of time. This - is the birth of heat:
The clemency of April - near to May -

Where bees attend to flowers - and assay -
Each grain of pollen. Life was never sweeter:

The nectars of tomorrow gild today
Where bluebells bud - and birdsong near completes -

The moment of the cuckoo's dual deceit
That drifts amongst the shadows: then decays.

COLD TEXT - WARM COLLATION

The crocuses have come: strangers in gold
Attire - giving the lie to this

Barren landscape. They are the kiss
Of spring - whisperers - of all that's told

Of light - where blackbirds try their voices -
Try to sing - and snowdrops say goodbye

To thoughts of ice. This blue - begotten sky -
Approaches bliss: where cumuli make choices

Of their own - cannot resist the gilding
Of the sun. Listen - and remember -

You're alive: the corpse of cold
December Is exhumed - revivified - by rills

And rivulets - that babble as they bloom
Across the hills. This is the time for love:

The budding of our purpose - and enough -
Where all the thoughts of darkness and our doom

Are lightened by the languages of birth.
The jasmine is an aureate collation:

Calligraphy - gold-leaf - on winter's pages -
That turns the text - from vagueness: into verse.

MIRAGE

I'm - for the moment - and the sun: tomorrow
Is a cold forgotten day - where swallows

Shun their pathways - and go south.
Today Is all I need: it's August - and the clay

Is cracked to fissures - and weeds - which I call
Flowers - tempt the bees. Butterflies are falling

Out of blue - chromatic snow - in drifts
Across the eyes - where larks are song and swifts

The screech of summer. The burnet moths and skippers
Skim the air - where light has turned to ripples

And the trees - are molten in the mirage
Of my mind. Though I am small - the world is large

Indeed - where sunshine stretches endlessly
Away - and my horizons - question -

All but time. Am I young - or old? The willow-
Pond reflects a distant dream: a pose

In nature's mirror - dark and deep - where crucian
Carp were gold beyond compare - and love a truth.

The thistledown - a blizzard - soft and rare:
An instant as the yellowhammer sings

Combining - now - both thoughts of here and there -
As cabbage-whites - like angels: spread their wings.

RIVER THURNE (Thurne, Norfolk)

A dyke - a church - a windmill and a pub:
What more is needed - surely its enough

To feed a man - both body and the spirit?
A heron stands in silence and aloof

As if in grey - his solitude - were proof
That all a being needs of wealth or wit

Is this long hour. The breezes scuff
The surface of the Thurne and sunlight touches

Substance - as it glitters. What more - I say -
What more: the harrier surveys the widening

Marsh - a law unto itself in skies
So faint that as it soars it almost fades

From view. The cattle move - like clouds through August
Heat: a bulk at once substantial - and a bluff -

That shimmers with a weightlessness - a glaze.
Such days are these when summer sets its sails:

When in the wake of water light regales
And coots obey - discordance - in the haze.

A dyke - a church - a windmill and a pub
And all the time - that's timeless: and enough.

SNOWDROPS BY THE RIVER (Ulting Church - Essex)

The snowdrops bunch and bloom on this green bank:
Purity and purpose in the sun - hankering

For summer and the bees. The snows - are done:
Whiteness - only flowers - and the frost

That coats the shadowed edges - to emboss -
Each blade of grass. My heart is overcome:

Reflections in the river - brim and bless -
The passing - cold - complexities

Of ice - that crystallize - like moments
In the mind. These flowers - just say yes:

A nodding thought - that here must acquiesce -
To spring's warm valediction to the snows

In blue and gold. Colour - has returned:
Has splintered through the prism of a birth

And turned - the wings of weather - into song.
These pallid bells that chime on every breeze:

This carillon - this silent - symphony -
Will sound the knell of winter - like a gong -

Where whiteness - rights all wrongs - on this green bank
And something thaws - and softens: like thanksgiving.

SONG OF OURSELVES

We are the blackbird's song: every cadence -
Every note - belongs - and all our tenses

Vanish with the music. We are the depth
Of spring: the warm - uplifted breath

That lights the sun - and brings to earth the crocus
And the squill. We are the will of God:

A thought revealed - a notion - something odd -
That fuels the rose and every budding moment.

Listen - to yourself: the mellow - fluted -
Resonance of light - dispelling at a glance

Your winter's heart - and giving life a chance
Beyond the stars. You do not need to choose:

The weather - though itself - expresses us -
Involves the wren - the robin - and the thrush

in such a song of infinite ideas
That we forget succession - and the years

Of our desires. Listen - to the choirs:
The harmonies - that link us - to the flowers -

As skylarks climb the bluff of every hour
And bless the Word - from blue: eternal spires.

STASIS

What do you know of time: when moments pass
Are you aware of love - where dandelions

Shimmer in the grass - and gold laburnum
Dazzles in the sun? Do you still ask

The meaning of the clock - when great-tits keep
The double beat of spring - and cuckoos sound

Antiphonal replies? The lilac's bound
To this repeated hour - that somehow creeps

Upon us every year: yet stays the same.
A blackbird flirts its metronomic tail:

Then opens wide its beak to here assail
The ramparts - given greenness - as a name.

Time - does not exist: each flower shows
A sequence as it blooms but bees insist

Eternity abides - as with a kiss -
They seed - tomorrow's vows. Even the rose

Is budding with the thorn: the scented - warm -
Serenity of light - will form in you

A stasis - still and calm - and slow the blue
Surrender of the skies. Think not of storms:

The swallows carry summer on their wings -
Unhurried - like wisteria - and heat

Where all the air holds fragrance while it breathes
And skylarks: are suspended - as they sing.

SONGS OF LIGHT

Songs - and the sense of summer: bees just hum
Their ground bass - on the wing - and blackbirds sing

In dark angelic choirs. I cannot bring
Myself to hear them all - those numberless

Equations of the year that here enthrall
The balance of the mind - and move the heart.

The chaffinch flakes each note to chips and sparks -
That dazzle down the lichen on the wall

And slake the sun. My thirst for song - is sated:
The robin - and the dunnock - and the wren

Add all they can of sanctus and amen -
To this warm psalm. Even the rose is weighted

By a sound: a sweet astounded resonance
In time that moves through heat with music -

Soft and slow - and stills all tense. We do not choose
The moment - or the mood - where fragrance

Lends its lyric to the air - and love inclines.
This symphony of summer is a gift:

An instant - like the swallow or the swift -
Where doves intone and drowsily define

Those deep encoded madrigals of light
That bless the ear - and flower: in the eyes.

I

I know this river well: formative - in
All that it reflects - a window

Without glass - where I must delve. I scry
My former years - and find the drifting sky

Is much the same - while I - am somehow different
And alone. The swallows and the swifts

Still skim my mind - but in this misted focus
Lies despair - as wind amongst the rushes

Sifts and sighs. The lily-flower - is gold:
But it can't speak - and I - am never told

The thoughts of time. The streamer-weed still sways:
An undulating memory of days -

Where I - was once the king of my desires.
Who is this I - I talk of - and require -

To see the roach and dace in silver seams
As if I had the will to work the dream

That once was mine? This mirror - doesn't lie:
The depths are dark - but nothing can disguise -

The shadows - as they shift - amongst the bream
And cloud the liquid vision of my eyes.

JANUARY THE SEVENTEENTH

A south-facing wall: and one - daffodil.
Almost all there is of spring - a solitary
Thought - a lingering question. What - will

Come to pass: will the bee find a haven
In this early flower - or the sun ignore
It as it melts the frost? These are the days

Between: each harbinger - a law
Unto itself - as isolation
Has no more to say - than winter's door

Has opened - is ajar. The earth has shown its will:
One bright idea - one transitory
Notion - that names itself: right now - a daffodil.

There are no songs - no fanfares in the score:
Just muted gold - and somehow: consolation.

THE ROSE AND THE NIGHTINGALE
(For Dylan Thomas)

The light inclines: but where I do not know -
For I am but my shadow in the sun
When near all else is gilded - like the rose -

With thoughts of love. The doves may drowse and sing
On staves of heat but all is dark in my
Heart's shaded bower and nothing brings

Contentment to my mind. The blackbird tries
But cannot reach the note when other things
Preoccupy my thoughts and sadness vies

With silence - and the bees. My shadow grows
As dusk envisions night and I am dumb
To speak the evening star. The light - declines and goes:

Save for the moon and one lone nightingale
Whose melancholy purpose - dims the roses.

REVELATIONS

Today I hear the rooks:
I look towards
The crown of every elm
And there they are
As raucous as the Book
That speaks of hell:
    I can't afford
The overwhelming
Thought that takes me far
From spring's own crystal brooks
To cross the Styx and hear that dreaded knell.

Today I see the crows:
I hear them go across
The fields of dusk
Towards the twilight roost
Of endless stars
And endless night:
Do you suppose I'm lost
Like this lone thrush
Who sings the fearful music
    Of the dark
And teeters on the brink of life and light?

The nightingale is mine:
The time that beats
With sorrow in the thorn
Where every note's
A feature of my heart
And love's unkind:
I can't conceive
Why I was ever born
To hear this midnight threnody - the throat:
That pulses with a purpose - like the stars -
When I am Blind.

SILKEN SHADOWS

The blackbird - calls alarm:
        Why
When the autumn sunlight
  Warms my mind
   I could not say.
    It is a psalm -
     The sky's
So blear - yet bright -
And to such fervent antics I am blind:
  Can see no harm.

The silence - is a choir:
        How
When the silken shadows
     Move my heart
    I cannot tell:
     Now
When the swallows
Haunt the distant past
And thoughts of frost and starlight ring the knell.
  Of my desires.

The mist - somehow beguiles:
        Why
When the spider's magic
  Speaks of death
   I could not say:
    The style
    Of this fly
  No less than tragic -
As every thought is ghosted by my breath
  And light's - on trial.

APPARENTLY

The bluebell woods are blue:
What else could they be?
Is truth as we see it
Or is there something
Hidden from our eyes -
Like God's own fire? The things I see
   Are witnesses
      Of love -
Dissemblers in the depths of a disguise
That say far more than all we could inquire
   Of form's illusion.

The daffodils are yellow:
Is that what we discover?
Are bees and blooms
A semblance - are they real -
These lurid shapes
That fanfare one-another
And cheat the eyes?
     Does love
       Assume
The cloak of the Ideal -
Or is the matter something that escapes
The mind - of both the sinner - and the lover
   And taints the rose?

CHILL BREATH

The easterlies are yours:
Cold as your eyes complain
   Of all I've done
Since summer and our love
Has turned to tears:
Is this a natural law -
Does winter suffer pain
  Without the sun
    When doves
      Are mute
Like our autumnal fears?
The leaves that fall are spring's unwritten spores
But your chill look has left me near insane -
  My heart refuted.

The trees are naught but bones:
Anatomies of stark
  Denuded hope
Where your rebuke
Is colder than the wind
And cloud despairs:
The pond will turn to stone
   And darkness
  Bring the ghosts
Of our warm youth
    Into the air:
I am no saint - believe me - I have sinned
But your reproachful silence and your glance
  Leave light disputed.

ASYMMETRY

Spatial awareness: something I lack - she said -
Not a failing - just a cerebral
Reality. Different sides of the head -

It seems - the opposite of verbal - a loss
Of innate geometry. She told me
To stick to words - that they were the gloss

On my neural network. Although I agreed -
She just wouldn't listen: got cross
When I spoke of love - the symmetry

Of heart - and all dimensions. I lost the thread:
My thoughts could not articulate the visual -
Could not imagine - anything - she said.

The patterns - like mosaic - misconceived:
Each piece - still unconnected: individual.

DAFFODILS (For Robert Herrick)

They speak - at last - of gold:
Unimaginable in winter
They take a hold
Of my inclement mind -
  New minted
  With a hint
Of things untold
And all the wealth of summer - unconfined.

They are the breath of stars:
Realisable in light
They warm my heart
With wonder - and the bees.
  Requited
  In the sight
Of time that passes
And just a thought of love - eternity.

They manifest devotion:
Intelligible in spring
They form a notion
Close to the divine -
  Birds singing
  Have the ring
Of rich emotion
And sunlight gilds the grass - the celandine.

SKYLARK

These are the wings of prayer: the lark ascends
The stairway of a song - and turns the air

From winter into spring. It has no care
For earth: it soars and sings - amens -

From such a height - that sound itself is muted -
Tinged with gold. I've never seen such light

Beneath the sun: such lyrical excitement
Under clouds - where whiteness touches blue

As love is sung - and all the dews of morning
Disappear. Such flight attains the apex

Of desire - as passion lets its lexicon
Of notes - to here conspire warmly

With the ear - and set the throat of summer
With its seeds. The corn - will surely grow:

Will claim its August voice - and one small shadow -
That scarcely moves - as music: lifts - and plumbs.

A SONG FOR EASTER

You - and the daffodil - are one: emblems
Of a moment in my mind - when spring
Becomes the semblance of our love. Remember
The ecstatic - the divine: the times
We had when blackbirds thought to sing
And God became an aspect of our hearts?
And even now the sunlight is sublime:
An alchemy - un-conjured - unsurpassed -

Where blossom shows its delicate design
And thrushes sing their madrigals of gold.
How glad I am that you are truly mine:
As constant as the crocus and the thrush
That yearly take the kernel from the cold
And warm our lives. I need - no more than this:
The passion of a flower as we touch
And God's - own resurrection: in a kiss.

THE LITANY OF SUMMER

Bread - and wine: sunlight and the roses
In the garden. Nature's humble access -
Where blackbirds - are forgiven - as they pose

And sing their subtle hymnal - to the skies.
Eucharist - is light: a transubstantiation
Through the leaves - a burning bush - a prize

That's cloaked in gold. What is - this covenant -
The body and the blood: the dragonfly
That hovers - like a cross - illuminant:

A pause - in earthly time? The mystery still shows:
The sermon of the bees - that buzz and bless -
Each sacramental flower - as it blows.

The litany is more than creed - or cant -
When doves - become petitions: and replies.

SWAN LAKE

Come to the dance - the waltz of this warm spring:
Where butterflies are practicing quadrilles
And all the birds - encouraged - thus to sing
Are unsurpassed. The swaying - but the daffodils
That dream: that fantasize on love and things

Of light where all that moves impinges on
The eye and primes the choreography
Of wings. Look to the lake - and the swans:
The *pas de deux* of whiteness on the breeze
Where each inverted image rights the wrongs

In winter's heart. The swallows also dance
Where water gleams: bow and lift across
The floor of glass where partners are a chance
That skim the sheen - and twirl on air. Our loss
Is that of ice as sunlight looks askance

And then redeems the moment with a kiss
Of molten gold. The arabesque - is held:
A stillness - and a purity - like bliss
Where butterflies and swallows mix and meld
And water - holds the chorus: is transfixed.

SUNLIGHT AND CELANDINE

Blessed are the celandine:
A sacrament of gold
And God's idea
Where light and time
Delimit winter's cold:
   The year
Now less severe
Warms every clime
Including this chill heart - as leaves unfold.

Glory - gilds the thrush:
The sanctity of song
Attunes the ear
And summer's hush -
As yet - does not belong:
   How clear
   The searing
Sound that heats the mind
And leaves the silent borders - long and lush.

The purpose is divine:
The wealth is sold
For nothing - but don't rush -
For sound and time
Will sanctify the ear:
   Gold
  Yes molten gold
  Will thus recline
And bees will touch the celandine - like tears.

SOUND AND SILENCE

The greenfinch wheezes: spring's excuse for
Song - when sunlight sings a music
Of its own - and silence fades. The rhythmic law

Of life begins anew: a pulse - the germ
Of birth in every sound as flowers
Crave attention from the bees and love's warm earth

Is woken by the thrush. Explore this golden hour:
Look for the leaves unfurling - in their search -
For summer and a lyric of such power

That proves the spheres symphonic - nothing more.
The blackbird's dark cadenza slowly soothes
The memory of winter - and its score -

Where nothing moved - like music in rehearsal -
And snow - was staves of crystal: muted showers.

BLUE EYES AT EASTERTIDE

Stay close my love - and live: forgive the many
Deaths that you have suffered - the times you've died
Because of my cold words. Come now - believe

In spring: come down the lane that's warming
In the sun - like my old heart. The lilac
And laburnum know the thrush - whose speckled form

Is pulsing with a song. These April skies -
Enamoured - know the passion - that formerly
Was ours and still could be if you and I

Were silent and forgetful. Your eyes do not deceive:
Though cool - they are as close - as Eastertide -
Where all the golden palm and love's own leaves

Have risen out of winter - and its tomb -
That we should kiss - like flowers: kiss the bees.

THE HEART'S INVESTMENT

The more you pay - the less you get:
If you invest in thought
And claim ideas
The slow returns of summer
    Will diminish
And leave you poor:
       Forget
     The thought
Of wealth - it's in arrears -
The swallow forks its tail and not its tongue
Where light becomes the meaning and the kiss
   Of nature's law.

The more you get - the less you pay:
The heart's returns
Believe me - are still free -
Where bees and flowers
Give without a thought
   And still the mind:
        Repay
      Your birth
Without your memory -
Rely for wealth on this unbroken hour
Where thrushes are a song that can't be bought
   And coins are blind.

DEPTHS OF BLUE

Look into the skies:
See where the sun
Disguises love with light
And all the stars -
Though hidden - are alive
With thoughts of fire:
    Do not rely
On vision - you're undone -
When you assess the moment with your sight
And not your heart:
    Do not strive -
Assume - or yet aspire -
When all you ask is golden in reply
And time burns bright with elements of wonder.

Look into the seas:
See where the waves
Dissemble and deny
The truth that's sounding
Deeply in the dark
Of your desires:
Do not believe
In silence - or the staves -
That hold the fish in love's
    Own thermocline
And light's cold ground:
    Do not ask -
Assume - or yet enquire -
When oceans keep their secrets as they sleep
And only ships - that founder: find a grave.

TADPOLES

The pond has come to life: after the frogs
The yellow-flags - spearing the sunlight
And the pear's white blossom. Time's cogs

Are set in motion: tadpoles and boatmen
Testing the meniscus - the viscosity -
Where things that sink or rise or gently float

Partake of light's inversion - and a tree -
That slowly drowns. The blackbird holds a note
That swims on air - where imagery

Is water and the sun and nothing bogs
The mind down: like a thought. Just sound - and sight:
Spring emerging brightly from the fog -

Where vision is a glint unwritten creed
And tadpoles - in parentheses: in quotes.

THE BLOSSOMING OF DEATH
(For Christina Rossetti)

Think not of me - I am not dead: my breath
Revives the wings of butterflies and spring
Is always open - like the tomb. What death:

What demon that dissembles and deludes
Could take me from your green remembering mind
That buds and flowers? You need no proof:

The sun and all the sympathy that shines
Cannot deny the beauty and the truth
When my own song inheres - and thus refines -

The blackbird's music. There's more than death - on earth:
The semblance is in essence all we sing -
Renewal - yes - renewal not just birth

Where I will live beyond the reach of time
In this one rose - that blesses: as it blooms.

REPRISE

Try to remember: not just the past
But the future - if past and future make
Any sense at all. There is sequence in the stars
Admittedly but nothing can take

The moment from itself - the eternal song
Of each unending second. The thrush's note
Compresses in the sun where blossom throngs
The instant of the pear and petals float

Like spectres on the breeze. This - is the death
Of time: where daffodils are motionless
With bees and April holds perfection - and its breath -
As light inclines. Remember - you are blessed:

The liturgy of love is this reprise -
This double note delivered by the thrush
That brings each passing moment to its knees
And counterpoints - infinity's: long hush.

CADENCES

Late April - red with tulips:
Heat for the bees
To enter and consume
Where love and light
Are pollen - and the kiss -
   Is one of fire:
      On knees
They find each bloom
   A sacred site
And every drone's - the ground bass: of a choir.

The pear - is white with blossom:
Rarity and reverence
For the thrush
Whose song is sung
In sunlight's - holy gloss -
As gold inspires:
   The tense
     Denies all hush
From spring's warm lungs
And every note - delivers: on desire.

The butterflies - are whispers:
Kaleidoscopes of colour
In the mind
Alighting on each
Flower - like a wish -
In love's attire:
   The lull
In sound defines
The grace they preach
And then they lift - and lazily: aspire.

LOVE SONGS AND SYRINGA

Believe me - this is love:
The crickets rub their legs
And all is passion
As sunlight fills the grasses
    With its gold
And hearts - are roses.

Listen - it's the thrush:
Its ardency is whitened
    By syringa
And every note is doubled
    - Like desire -
In summer's furnace.

Listen - hear the doves:
They do not care for fashion
    - Or the clegs -
When cumuli are bold
And light surpasses
What we suppose.

Believe me - it's not lust:
The moment is enlightened
    As we linger
Beneath the leaves untroubled
    By a fire
That will not burn.

IF (For Rudyard Kipling)

If there is glass in your heart
- Deny it -
Believe in blood
When crystal has congealed
That you may see transparently
For once
And feel emotion.

If there is ice in your eyes
 - Control it -
Believe in light
When frost has locked your soul
That you may touch the tenderness
That thaws
And knows devotion.

If there is stone in your voice
- Erode it -
Believe in speech
That reasons and reveals
That you may break the scree of your
Hard words
When love is spoken.

CAN IT BE SAID?

The thrush tries out his song
And flakes of snow
Drift down like fallen notes
Between the branches:
Can it be said
That crystal chills the heart
When such as he
Has fire in his lungs
And blood that quickens?

The snowdrops nod in throngs
As if they know
By reason and by rote
And not by chances:
Can it be said
As frost entombs the grass
That such as they
Are conscious of the sun
When snow still thickens.

The weather has its wrongs:
The wind that blows
May freeze the blackbird's throat
But light enhances:
Can it be said -
Though water turns to glass -
That such as I
And crocuses are dumb
As winter - sickens?

PHASED BY MOONLIGHT

The moon was in the west
- Almost northwest -
Stars were flecks of ice
Between the clouds
And time was blown
On skeins of winter geese
Towards the marsh.

The saltings were a guess
- All dressed in white -
Where snow had left its shrouds
On silts and sand
And curlew curved across
   the distant bars
With ghosts of song.

Do we belong to weather
   such as this:
Where seas are sown
With sequins made of frost
And light that leaves
The precincts of the land
Is lost amongst the shadows
   and the sighs
Of tides - that splinter?

WHITE-OUT AT BARLING MAGNA

Winter - bites back:
The westerlies concede defeat
And down the air
Siberia descends
In wisps of whiteness:
The sky is black -
Like thoughts of pitch
Without attendant heat -
Where winter's lens
Illuminates the sightless
With glints of crystal.

Hedgerows thicken:
The chaffinch and the robin
Sear with red
As berries burn and blister
In the cold
And ice enlightens:
Nothing -quickens -
The snowdrops nod
Their acquiescent heads
Where crocuses resist
All thoughts of gold
And water - quietens.

ICE AND THE EVENING STAR

Only the trees complain:
Everything else is whitened
By the weight
Of muted crystal:
The wind will not be silenced -
It wails its banshee words
Through hedge and wires
As lapwings make
Their journeys further south
And winter - thickens.

Only the moon is sane:
It rises into twilight
Through the gates
Of clouded vistas:
The stars abhor such violence -
They watch the weather's curse
Yet still aspire
While foxes shake
Their victims in their mouths
And venus - sickens.

FEBRUARY THRUSH

Ice on the pond:
Leaves, furred at the edges
And a song thrush
Singing:
Is there any need
For spring?
These songs that melt
The hoar frost on the hedge
Are just as lush
As all that
May can bring -
The seed
Is sown in winter
- like a wedge -
A cold - beginning.

SIGNS

There are certain signs
- Symbols -
Like violets with sweetness
On their minds -
Where crocuses and coltsfoot
Lift their heads
To see if they can see
The pure design
Of sunlit - sigils.

There are certain gyres
- Gimbals -
Like cycles that repeat
- When they're inclined -
    To write
Such hieroglyphics in the beds
Of snowdrops that increase
  As they define
Their winter's - vigil.

ZERO AND BELOW

Suppose if you will
That frost is as thick
As a fall of snow -
That ice on the pond
Blocks entry to the moon
And that stars are as sharp
As needles tipped with diamonds.

Think - if you can -
Of a fox as quick
As zero and below -
That blood is a bond
Only death can choose
And that ways are dark
With shadows - ferns and fronds.

Walk - if you will -
Where trees are sticks
Turned silver - somehow lunar -
Where light beyond
Is silent -just a glow -
And the cold is as black
As beetles - deep and still.

SPOKEN

The chaffinch speaks:
Staccato words
That rattle into spring -
Where crocuses reply
Through gapes of gold
And magpies - chatter.

What can we say
When sunlight finds its voice -
When winter's muted moment
    Is undone
And all the woken choirs
  Of the birds
Uplift - their praises?

April turns to heat:
A warming verse
Of light and other things -
Where daffodils contrive
To kill the cold
As pollen - scatters.

What can we say
When spring becomes a noise -
When frost in dumb atonement
    Greets the sun
And all the leaves transpire
    As they learn
Their gilded - phrases?

MELTING SNOW

Why do I stand in the snow:
Hold out my hands
Like some excited child
As manna falls
From heaven and affirms
My deepest - wishes?

I suppose that I should grow old:
Be more relaxed,
More sensible and calm
As winter flows like ice
Along my veins
And time - unfreezes.

Why should I hope for zero:
Desire lands
Where whiteness has grown wild -
Where light recalls
The past in its own terms
And frost - was kisses?

Why was it all untold:
Now that I track
The weather in my palms -
Where snow must pay the price
And melt - like rain -
As age increases?

SUNDIAL

There is no room for sadness. The robin
Sings his melancholy song but snowdrops

Shake their heads - like a denial -
And missel thrushes counteract the storm

With lungs of fire. The sunlight brings
Its boon through rifts of cloud where summer's ghost

Contends - and yet conspires - to smile
On the absences of light. The formless

Will revive: the south return on wings
Embossed with gold as daffodils compose

Themselves in heat - in spring's own style.
There is no need for sadness - time will warm -

As swallows thread their pearls along the strings
Of looping wires. Summer will suppose

What we assume when cuckoos count on guile
With a song - that gilds the corn. It is the norm -

Believe me: trust in the ways of spring.
The robin's song may speak of winter's woes

But crocuses are gnomons on the dial
And even shadows: shimmer - as they're born.

BEYOND THE GLARE

I'm not used to London:
The people after midnight
   On the streets -
The neon lights - the inviolable traffic.

Canals are interesting though:
Reflected stars
Buried in velvet -
A robin - innocently - singing
By the towpath -
The moon in purdah.

It's the continual hum
That gets me:
A noise that isn't quite
   A noise -
An inexorable something
Like the workings
Of a vast machine
Grinding the granite
Of unyielding pavements.

In the less frequented corners
- Down mews and alleyways -
I can see the iridescence
   Of the stars -
The moon above darkening spires.

But something moves me onwards
To the outskirts:
The sports fields and the Lombardy's
   Quick-silvered -
Where owls are known
To offer up their wisdom
And even night
Has shadows to believe in
- Beyond the glare.

JANUARY FOG

Have you ever felt
That when you express the weather
It's the weather expressing you?

Strange that the fog is so obscure:
That dew-point can eliminate all distance -
Reduce perspective.

There's something vague about the trees:
Leafless and indeterminate -
Like thoughts in the neural network
Veined and branching into grey dimensions.

That crow with a shaft
Of sunlight on his shoulder:
Is he the devil or an angel -
A dank and dark diminishment of daylight
Or just the cold negation of ideas?

He moves and the droplets
Shower me with silver:
Am I awake or adrift
In a dream's miasma?

My thoughts are blear:
My mind - but condensation.

Am I only left with monochrome and silence:
A weather eye - the dampness - obfuscation?
Although I look for something to hang onto
The world I know - and knew - just disappears.

UNDERGROUND MOVEMENT

The snowdrops lift their heads:
They whisper in their whiteness
- As the thrush -
Tunes up the trill
That warbles into spring
On this cold day.

They nod as in approval
   - So it's said-
When crocuses delight
In this slow rush
That climbs the hill
Of gold - and other things -
With thoughts of May.

The snowdrops lift their heads:
Purity - betrothal -
In the hush
Where winter finds the wisdom
   And the will
To listen to the latency that sings
Beneath - the clay.

AFTER THE RAIN

Come to me now in the rain:
When the spectrum bends
Through pure, prismatic crystals
And love is possible.

Your loss is mine as well:
Together we will scry
The hanging droplets
That cling - like silver sunsets -
    to the branches
And bleed with images.

Listen, love - the thrush
Revives our music:
Repeating notes
As we repeat our lives
In spring's upheaval.

The lake is stippled with light:
    mercurial beads
That bounce and then reverberate -
Ripple - with concentricity.

Radiate - my love - radiate:
Touch now the shores
With celandine and violets -
Where doves dispense with language
    for a song
And sunlight - glitters.

SUMMER'S END

In the quiet, the still
And the quiet
Of a summer afternoon -
I think of you
And all our time together -
Of all those days
Of doves and sounding heat
When you repeated vows
We never made
As flowers kissed
The countenance of bees
And I in love
With lyrics and the roses
Addressed your eyes.

Can I compete with time
When time has passed -
When evening comes
With twilight and the stars
And scented stocks
Remind me - and the moths -
That sweetness is a moment
   In the mind
That stills the heart?
Believe me love
As swallows string the wires
Like pearls on summer's necklace
Come September:
That I will banish autumn -
   Will remember
Those August fires.

CROCK OF GOLD

Have you seen the celandine -
The sunlight in the semblance of a flower
As bees assay the seams of early spring
    And riddle pollen?

    This hour is enough -
There is no bluff, no rusted, old pyrites
Where newly minted petals proffer wealth
With all the gold largesse of warming soil
    And precious songs.

Have you ever heard such ore:
Such notes so mined from darkness with a power
That realigns the sepals and the sight to times long passing?

An aureate eternity of love
Where collared doves cast decibels of sound
Like ingots in the lyrics of the trees
And molten leaves are fluid in the bud
Of all that stirs as rainbows bend their showers
    Towards the earth.

DECEMBER THE 27th

The birdbath's frozen over
And a robin sings
Its sad and northern song:
December moves towards
    A cold New Year
And night is on the cusp of my chill heart
As starlight splinters:
    Do you suppose
That angels have warm wings
When January breathes its ghostly wrongs
And all the sward is whiteness and severe?
Remember now as Christmas sidles past
That we will know the hoarfrost and the snows
    Of our long winter.

DECEMBER DUSK

The crows traverse the fields:
Black and heavy pinioned -
The only thoughts
Between me and the woods.

Trees are anatomical:
 Stark, bare,
Bones on the broken skyline -
Arthritic hands
Clutching at nothing.

Fieldfares plunder the hedgerows:
Ingest the blistering blood
Of hips and haws -
Stoke their December fires.

Pheasants are exotica:
Colour in a world
Made monochrome -
Indian princes
Invited by the Raj
To hunt the fox,
The roebuck and the hare.

The crows settle in the trees:
Cling to the sticks of winter
As the moon
Invests the calm
With silence - deep as frost -
Where one lone star,
A crystal, wrapped in velvet,
Envisions sound
As icy - as an owl's.

PATIO WINDOW

A fox was framed in darkness
  - We in light -
And I could sense
A semblance in our minds
Where eye meets eye
And thoughts, however different,
Assess each other.

The air, at least,
  Is mutual:
In this respect we breathe
And breathe to live
Where starlight is a code
That builds all flesh
And primes the heart.

The snow was falling fast
- And all was heat -
Where we in the domestic
Hearth of fire
Knew blood that warmed the moment
- Like the sun -
And he, or her,
For love - or yet - desire
Looked in upon his kindred
  Fallen angels
With eyes - like ice.

INGATESTONE - ESSEX

On every wall a lighted Christmas tree:
Ingatestone believes in love -
Knows Advent as the coming of the Lord.

Santa Claus and tinsel
Have their place
But country folk
Know shepherds and the ox
As one lone star drifts high above the farms
To herald more than commerce and a feast
    In time's constraints.

On every door a welcome and a wreath:
Ingatestone proclaims the Holy Dove -
Knows frost as the enlightenment of sward.

The fir tree's glittering winter
    Has its grace
But more is opened
Here than card or box
As blackbirds chink through twilight's icy calm
And snowflakes bring their worship from the east
    Like crystal saints.

BASIS

The lark is singing:
A dark lone star
In realms of blue
Where gold is the perception
   On the wing
And sound thanksgiving:
Where is the heart
Of such sweet music?
The score knows other regions of conception -
Other songs that sanctify and sing
The soul's own language.

The lark's suspended:
A lone dark angel
In realms of light
Where love is the reflection of each note
That hangs in stasis:
   The angle
   Of my sight
Beholds perfection -
Where every sound that leaves the lover's throat
Is never forced - or fathomed - or contended
With light - the basis.

SUMMER RIVER

Turn again to the river: to the blood
That flows unending to the sea, where

Fish are thoughts that swim between the weeds
And images are captured in the glare.

Look to the summer sunlight as it floods
Where loosestrife climbs to kiss the ardent bees

Before it delves. Come - have you felt the air:
The pollen and the perfume known as love

Where lilies lift their chalices - like prayer -
And doves: can only bring you - to your knees?

WINTER BERRIES - SPRING FLOWERS

Snow - turns back to rain:
The whiteness and the wonder
Disappear
And once again the world
Assumes its stance
Of browns and greyness:
The trees complain
About the lack of sunlight
As this new year
    Is hurled
Into the dance
Of wind and clay:

Snow - turns back to rain -
The fieldfares take their plunder
    And we fear
The may will keep its pearls
And never blanch
Except to prove that winter's clotted blood
Denies - the faithless.

TRINITY
The Christmas rose resembles that lost star
That used to shine in my untutored heart
When time was young. The fir is brought indoors
And 1 can smell the season and the shores

When those three ships came sailing in the sun
To herald dawn, and birth, and light, and love
In that far place. The wisest men I knew
Were overcome by thoughts that touched on truth

Beyond the grave - and desert sands. Believe
In threes - especially three in one - when reason
Is supplanted by the heart and Christmas
Roses, frankincense and myrrh, are gifts

Of gold. The Christmas rose dissembles:
Obscures the past - is nothing but an emblem -
When I would feel and readily depart
From realms of thought: to starlight -that surpasses.

MAY

Remember the thorn that flowers:
The blossom turning April into May
Where cuckoos call
Across the fields of rape
And swifts return
To scythe the warming air
    On sickle wings.

Remember the sun and showers:
The blackbirds singing sweetly on the spray
Where bluebells sprawl
Like sky in every glade
And tulips burn
In summer's early flare
With light that stings.

Remember the golden hours:
The petals and the pollen and the hay
Where skylarks stall
On songs that float and fade
And bees relearn
The perfume and the prayer
    Of all that sings.

OTTERS

The otters are back in the river:
Sleek and furred and sinuous
They break the surface skin
Of summer light
And dive for darkness.

Loosestrife are their torches:
Purple flares that delve
The flowery depths -
Where fish patrol the precincts
    Of a dream
Like silver shadows.

The otters are back in the river:
Cute - and yet - carnivorous
They calculate each fin
With perfect eyes
And kill - regardless.

Lilies watch their sorties:
Golden orbs unconscious of themselves
That pay the debt
Of sunlight, pure, succinct -
Where love is less than it should surely seem
    Beneath the willows.

BLOSSOM TIME

It's blossom time again:
The blackbird basks in whiteness
  On the bough
And claims once more
Its equinoctial rights
With drafts of song.

The chaffinch turns its breast
As pink as petals
Where mimic snow
Or spring's downthrown confetti
Illuminates the season
  And the lawn
With fallen stars.

The daffodils declaim:
Address the breeze that's brightness
  As it soughs
And frame the law
Of love and endless light
Where it belongs.

The sun is surely blessed
- As are the nettles -
Where butterflies are blown
And all that's petty
Is left to realms of reason
  And the form
Of time that passes.

WRENS AND ROSES

Have you heard the sound
  of summer
And the thrush
Where love alights
With sun-shafts in the trees
And leaves become a lyric
Green and gold
In June's warm song?

Do you believe the doves
  that serenade
Where light and shade
Are byways for the bees
And time's a panegyric
Blue and bold
Through golden clouds?

Can you not see the shifting
Of the shrouds
As skylarks climb
On madrigals of air
To lift the lilt of love
  so long untold
    into the skies?

Can you not hear the blackbird
  and the wren
Where time relies
On roses in its hair
To scent the sounding spirit
  of the doves
With light and longing?

COLLARED DOVES

The collared doves are singing:
January, dark and dawning cold,
Yet these warm hearts
Are breaking into song
Where winter jasmine
Constellates with stars
And light - conspires.

There is a fire in the south:
The Southern Cross is blazing
- High and hot -
But even yet the snow
Affronts the north
With lungs of ice.

The collared doves are singing:
January, chill and dawning white,
Yet crocuses are stirring
    In the earth
Where snowdrops hang their heads
Against the blast
And sound - aspires.

DO NOT DESPAIR

See now the crocus
   And the squill -
Where light descends
   Its February stair
Like spring's own angel.

Do not despair of love -
The song thrush sings
Eternally of hope
Where sunlight warms
The brimstone and the dove
   In this cold hour.

Hear now the cricket
And the lark
As if all winter's
Darkness turns to gold
   In August fires.

Do not despair of frost -
The will is there
To gild the hidden corn
And loss will find
The nectar and the bee
   In every flower.

MIRROR IMAGE

Did you see the snowdrops
Beside the river?
Reflected whiteness's
Quivering in the
January wind
Like purity excited
To be freed
From depths of darkness.

The river takes them in:
Releases them from earth
And frosted air
Where in the deeps
A clear, inverted warmth
Ignites the image.

Spring at last
Delivered from the soil
Because of love
Or some-such
Warm abstraction -
Will hold the eye
In aspic - like an icon -
Where fish are sudden
Miracles that swim
Between the clouds.

A LACK OF SYMBOLS

I am looking for signs of spring: symbols
Of warmth and sunlight as winter clings

With frost to every branch and blackbirds brood
In silence - hunched and starving. The music

That I need is still unsung where snowdrops
Sleep in slumberings of white and moments

Pass - eternally - in ice. Listen - if you must:
You will not hear the chaffinch or the thrush

As this cold day moves closer to the stars
And thoughts of night. There is silver in the grass:

Not treasure - or the lining of a cloud -
But steel that makes a mockery of vows

When winter's chill betrothal turns to bone
And even light: is less - than love's atonement.

SNOW AND SHADOWS

The snow is blown by the wind:
Roads become the fluid beds
  Of vapour -
Where whiteness flows
In currents made of ice
And midnight sparkles.

The moon and stars join in:
Are something said
Between the clouds that caper
Where light that glows
 Delivers its device
   - Like a debacle -

The snowflakes spread their wings:
Liquidity is shed
Like frozen paper -
Where winter knows
The purpose and the price
Of ink - that darkens.

A TEMPORAL ARRANGEMENT

Truth is more that beauty - more than joy:
The maggot and the canker and the worm
Are also part of this divided earth
And all it holds. The angels have a voice
That speaks two tongues - two separate meanings.
Each coin of light that fathoms from the trees

Has different sides - or shadows - even choices
That are not free. You can enjoy the storm
Or loathe the calm: the winter has its birds -
The summer hail - the equinox, its poise.
There are it seems no absolutes - just leanings -
And even flowers: presuppose - the bees.

A ROSE FOR SIRIUS

A yellow rose -
Amongst the autumn leaves:
  a memory
Of summer in the sun
When all the gold and scarlet
Would deceive
With thoughts of fire:
Nothing grows
But embers
  of desire -
Where this lone flower resurrects the star
That summer knew - ascendant - in the heat
Of larks and doves.

A yellow rose -
Amidst the autumn frost:
A semblance
  of July
In cold November
When lapwings fly - like semaphore -
  in blue
And mist transpires:
There is no loss
This emblem
Burns the eye -
Where light inclines and shadows can't dissemble
The constellated petals in the score
Of sound's - translucence.

DOVES AND DARKNESS

Paradise is yours:
Remember all you know
Of autumn mists
Where insubstantial thoughts
And shapeless forms
Configure into trees
And flighting birds
Before your eyes.

The toadflax is a door:
A lambent glow
That's bordering on bliss
Where nought
Is somehow born
- Somehow perceived -
And thought becomes
The long-forgotten word
Where nothing dies.

The garden is sublime:
November is the fire
  In your heart
Where fallen fruits
    Ferment
And thought aspires
On draughts of love.

The starlings
Are but angels made of time:
Charred photons of desire
  Seeming dark
Where winter's roots
    Relent
And light conspires
To gild the doves.

UNION

Is the falling leaf aware:
Does it know itself
As part of light's exchange
Where love is turned
From star-shine into stone
And living flesh?
Is there thought in this cold air:
Are the many deaths
Of God so rearranged
That emptiness still yearns
The blood and bone
Of endless wealth?

How can I still despair?
Beneath the naked trees
I walk through gold
Where years of light
And darkness disappear
   into the earth.
Our mother breathes and cares:
   She is the She -
The womb of all foretold
Where He we know as starlight
   stills our fears
With seeds of birth.

TIDAL

Come to the moon - the magic of the night -
Where sentences are silver and the stars

Repeat your words. The owl is but a ghost
Who you believe - its haunted voice consoles

As it condemns and you will know the wisdom
Of its claws. See more than mere Polaris

And the dark: the tide reflects both starlight
And the void and you will know in emptiness

The light - that does not shine. The curlew flutes:
Its syllables are ghosted on the night

Where spectres are the fogbanks and the geese
That form and fade from substance - like a thought -

That comes and goes. Orion takes his stride:
He moves across the constellated dream

Where winter speaks with fires made of frost
And darkness - somehow dazzles - though you're blind.

Come to the moon - the mystery of light -
Where time and tide repeat the soundless voice

And you - are no more you - than I am I -
Except where waves bring semblance to our shores.

THE SKYLARK'S GOLDEN SONG

Paradise to me: this one small garden
Satisfies my needs when blackbirds call
And thrushes make reply and all the stars
Of stitchwort make amends for winter's thrall
And memories of ice. What's past is past:
The butterflies - reborn - remove the pall

As resurrective flowers claim the bees
And blossom glimmers. White light has found
The prism of a shower and time's reprieve
Is spectral - summer's ghost - in April's clouds.
The chaffinch is a fire that believes -
A sudden spark that startles, like a vow,

When sunlight powers more than scent or sap
Amongst the trees. The cherry and the pear
Are holy now, as if all thoughts of matter
Were refined, to whiteness - like a prayer,
On every bough - in every heart. Perhaps
I fool myself: believe that all despair -

That all the dark - is passing with the promise
Of the rose. A greenfinch - trills and wheezes:
The thought of heat is sentient and strong
And I cannot condemn when all conceives:
The world is like a psalm - a sacred song -
And collared doves: bring joy - although they're grieving.

I am no fool: the daffodils are gold
As is the palm and Easter finds the passion
And the Goddess - to be but one. How old
Is spring - or love? These names are more than fashion.
The skylark's wings unfurl as leaves unfold
And every note: upholds - the rationale.

MISTLETOE AND IVY

The first Sunday in Advent and the loft
Reveals its treasures: tinsel and lights -
A synthetic tree - baubles and frosted

Banners. Ritual revisited: white
Thoughts at the blackest time of year when holly
Sheds its blood and every thorn's enlightened

By the fantasy of snow. We will be jolly:
Rest assured that Santa Claus will come
And we will know - no more - the former folly

That chilled our hearts. 'Peace on earth' - the sun -
'Good will to men'. Remember love - the poor -
The dispossessed when in the woods the running

Of the deer - leaves tracks and shadows. It thaws
The mind: this memory of something
Not quite known, when partridges adore

The realms of song and all the bells are ringing -
Clear as stars. The past is undefined:
A dream to cling to. We need this thing

Called love: this thought that ivy twining
Round the oak - will never strangle. 'Gloria
In Excelsis Deo' - 'Blessed be' - 'Thine

Is the Kingdom'. The Passion has its gore:
But Christmas and the solstice speak of birth
When all is death and darkness to the core

Of our cold earth. What is this universe:
This portent that implores the seeming wise
To follow hope and see in time some worth?

The golden bough holds kisses at a height
And we will reach: or pray - or symbolise.

SIMPLE THINGS

Simple things. The wren's familiar voice:
Celandine in sunlight - crocuses - the first
Butterflies. We have no earthly choice,

These are the ways of spring: singing birds -
Flowers that tempt the bees, and all that time
Can muster from the dark where light and words

Are limitless - like love. Some say - sublime:
Others - a curse. What to me returns,
And always will, is nothing but a crime

To those who mourn - or suffer pain. The verse
A celebration or a dirge? Attitudes
Of mind - viewpoints - beliefs. Listen to the birds -

They sing despite themselves. The light accrues
By increments - a song - as flowers bend
The spectrum to their will and all assumes

The aspect of a prayer - some frail amen.
Complexity asserts itself: no more
The black and white of winter trees - the end

Of every answer is at hand where spores
And seeds pose questions for the sun - and sap
Must quicken. What is it - nature's law:

A certainty - a semblance - a perhaps,
Where we assess the darkness and the dove
As seasons turn and something seems to happen?

The celandine have bees and that's enough
For this small heart to pollinate a wonder.

GREEN PLOVERS (Freezing Fog, River Crouch, 2005)

The plovers range across the winter wheat
As fieldfares chack and redwings catch the sun
In looping flight. The residues of heat
Are here expunged as frost alone becomes

The only word - to freeze the mind. Berries
Are the blood the hawthorn needs to prime
The heart of zero with a thought that feeds
The spring. The plovers - rise as one - and time

Becomes a semaphore of wings where blue
And black and whiteness are the creed and light
Ascribes its cipher to the soul. What truth
Is there in substance? What beauty lies

In seeing? What about ice? This puddle
Once was water - once was air: but now
We know solidity it seems - and mud
Is stone. Confusion. Tonight the Plough

Will turn around Polaris and in the Crouch
The galaxies will drown - the moon subside.
Now geese draw out their skeins along the reach
And like the hounds of hell their voices chide

All thoughts of love. I am speechless - with my speech:
The plovers dip and dive and sometimes cry
As if they know - and even dare to vouch -
That what I see is semblance - but a lie.

The sun sinks down - is done. Venus shivers.
A shelduck laughs and I must wonder why
As cold-condensing air and all that glimmers
Is shrouded - insubstantial - undefined.

The rime lays down its reasons on the thorn
And tides will turn: and daylight - bring the morning.

CURLEW AND CUMULI

Not to everybody's taste - this flat
And open landscape by the sea. The clouds
Are its only hills and all that matters
To the mind are those so solitary sounds

That curlew make and lapwings rend on air.
The saltings sift and sigh where grasses
Echo something of the tide and prayer's
A susurration over silt. The past

I must deny - the future also: now
Is of the instant and itself as geese
Assess the strata's of the sky and showers
Build their monuments to God. These mountains

Made of vapour, edged with ice, are passing -
Yet not passing - as they form, and something
Somehow whispers - there on high - of vastness
In the gulls' metallic seams. Even the sun

Is salted and preserved: all meanings
Are reduced to this wide marsh where flatness
Is eternal in its guise and single trees
As arbitrary as time. Where now - the pattern?

The heron stands as still and grey as stone
As this eroded moment turns to sand
And light diffuses silver in my bones.
Why try, why even think to understand?

The redshank are released from heaven's bow
And all is sound: and silence - and unknowing.

LION HOUSE

I can be covetous: Lion House -
A strange name for a dwelling, in an even
Stranger place. Barely an eminence, surrounded

By corn and saltings. I can believe
In something when I'm here - perhaps everything.
The sea-scented air whispers in the trees:

Oak and ash and fir, and all the singing
Birds that farmland yields. A yellowhammer
Wheezes in the heat and I can only think

A thoughtless thought where light and summer
Shimmers in the fields - and time stands still.
The butterflies uphold their August banners

As lavender from gardens and the silts
Pervades the mind - as substance-less as sky -
And primes the heart. An egret works its stilts:

A circus act that teeters into white
Where wormwood in this fire seems like frost
And asters are a smoke that will not rise

To greet the stars. A place of love - and loss:
My dreams are here - yet dreams - unrealised.
The curlew fall in vast migrating flocks

That hold the northern moorlands in their cries
And winter in the compass of their wings.
What can I do when homeless - but aspire:

Look out through eyes - like windows fit for kings -
And see beyond the mortar and the brick.
The light's horizon softens as it sings

And I am here: though absent - there's the trick
That conjures gulls, the skylarks, and my witness.

INNOCENCE REGAINED

The back-path was my paradise:
Every season had its angels -
Butterflies in spring -
Doves in the deepest summer
Warm with sound
And burnet moths
With bright empurpled wings.

Autumn had its leaves:
Ethereal feathers
Shaken through the mist -
Seraphim and cherubim
Gilding the faded moment
Like text in a sacred book.

Winter was frost and snowflakes:
Powers and Principalities
  made of ice -
Haloes round the moon
  and holy stars
Piercing the heavens
With their iridescence.

Paradise indeed:
Scuffed knees and birdsong -
Giant elms, and newts
In brimming ditches
Breaking the surface
With their crests on fire.

It's there - although it's not:
My memory still moves
Me through the trees
Where nightingales and owls
Enlighten darkness
And the Thrones of a distant day
Exalt the heights
Angelically - with thrushes.

SLASHER MARTIN

He could fish that man:
Could scan the river
With his laser eyes
And highlight dace
And roach in silver seams.

Ghosts of the deeps
Were more than apparitions:
Perch and bream,
Chub and pike -
Spectres that materialised
    at will.

He had the Midas touch:
Could fill his net with gold -
Gild his tongue with stories
    tall or long.

He probably bluffs St Peter -
Confounds him with his fishy miracles.

Ethereal rivers will not be safe:
He will sound the starlit streams
For trout and grayling:
Tench with eyes like suns -
Carp in the cloisters
Of the Milky Way.

I cast this float for him:
The next quicksilver roach
That takes my bait
Will not be flesh or bone
Or even matter:
It will partake of spirit
    - will connect -
The master and disciple
    - once - forever.

THE NIGHTINGALE AND THE ROSE

Love - what is it? The bees who kiss the flowers?
Tears from April skies? Rainbows? The clouds

Are as white as doves and orange-tips
Are dancing by the verge as if the lips

Of sunlight touched their wings. Enamoured
By the blush of early blossom a rampant

Thrush seems more attuned to lust; but swallows
Glance in mirrors and espy the followers

Of Venus - in reverse. April's cuckoos
Double their deceit and someone else's truth

Will be denied - the faithful rose. Love
Or lust? Eros or agape? Enough

Of hate lay frigid under snow - let hares
Revive and box across the fields as air

Uplifts on thermals and aspires
Towards the sun. Faithfulness? Desire?

How can we tell what's best when we're undone
And passions rise - like sap - in summer's

Veins? The turtle has returned and we should
Listen now to its own truth that fills the woods

And builds a nest for lovers. Love - what is it?
A calumny for those who steal; a kiss

When someone's hope had settled on the stars.
Remember this - when light is unsurpassed:

The nightingale - though fated by tradition -
Still courts the moon: with madrigals - not sadness.

FROZEN (Paper Mills - River Chelmer)

There is ice above the lock: the bothy
And the stables know the chill as memory

Is haunted by the toll of ghostly hooves.
Today is white and blue and passing truth

Returns another age when working men
Weren't spectres on this path and round the bends

The ropes would stretch and bow. How many loads -
How many bargee's lives - have made their slow

Progression from the sea between the reeds,
The rushes, and the lilies? But now - we freeze:

The fish are held in aspic and the ducks
Can only feed on handouts - luckless

Fowl. A barge would break the barriers of ice:
Would bring its bluff debacle to our eyes

And shatter time. Does water hold the past?
Does risen air condense beneath the stars

And hold a dream? Do absent swallows
Fathom other skies where water follows

On in tropic clouds and thunder captures
Horses - and their brass? Maybe - or just perhaps:

For now the misted mirror - silver cast -
Hides secrets: and clay pipes - in tides of darkness.

BREAM (Hoe Mill - River Chelmer)

The mill pond holds such bream: such golden slabs
Of scaly luminescence that all my dreams
Are delving in the depths of some perhaps -
Or thermocline of treasure. Subconscious seams
Of sunlight in the gloom: the fabulous
In layers - stratified - like endless reams

Of gilded, secret, paper. Archetypal
Images of light that I through the collective,
Cold, Unconscious, can see within the nightscape
Of my soul. They are not earthed - electric
Form and fin: as sinuous and writhing
Down the dark as lightning in the spectra

Of my mind. I mine the shafted darkness
With ideas and all the totem wishes
Of my tribe are focused on the strata's
Of a prayer. All thought - is shamanistic:
The silent deeps are golden and apart
And I: must plumb beneath - for love's own fishes.

SNOWY WOODS (For Robert Frost)

The snow comes down in veils: enormous flakes
That sidle through the trees where silence
Is a sense of something else that makes
The breath as eerie as a ghost. Ascendance

Is unheard of in these woods as darkness
Falls and moonlight through the clouds - is caught
And caged. Uncanny - this: these double stars
Of crystal - and of gas - where heaven sports

Its share of iridescence and earth
Attains a sparkle made of ice. The quiet
Is undone. Of all the sleeping birds
The robin wakes and makes a riot

Of its song. I cannot stay - it's late:
The badger and the fox have found their beds
And I must leave for home through this cold gate
Where light is lost: and snow so soft - and shedding.

ADLESTROP - OR ULTING?

Adlestrop - or Ulting? No trains, admittedly:
But summer and the country holds a sense
Of something shared - like flowers share the bees
Down this old lane. The light is so intense

I scarce can see but blackbirds sing and thrushes
Make reply as lone white clouds evaporate
In blue. No-one comes and no-one rushes
Through - in this still place. I am in isolation -

And in grace - as swallows glance the river
By the church - and loosestrife delves. June, July
Or August - all the same: the heat delivers
Images in glass of summer skies

And demoiselles reflected. Adlestrop -
Or Ulting? It matters not. Willowherb
And mallow here conspire to stop
The clock and gild the open lily as birdsong

Touches Essex - and the shires. Infinity?
It's burnished in the meadows and the fields
As skylarks climb and thrushes make reprise
Through every thought: and timelessness - unyielding.

ENLIGHTENED

The sun uplifts its erubescent head
Like some old agriculturist who peers
Above the hedge. I see the passing years
In its warm stare - as light and shadow stretch

Across the land - and speak of time. Tomorrow
Never comes - or so it's said - but now
Seems both the future and the past as ploughland
Lends perspective to the eye and furrows

Meet infinity - and mist. A blackbird sings
And I can hear the music of the spheres
In every note - in every cadence. Fear
Is all there is: unless you watch the winging

Of the swifts and see them veer across
The velvet lake - with dual reflections. Double-ness,
Division, two in one: light assesses
Spirit and the flesh when each is lost

To delving in the depths. The sun contracts
And brightens: illuminates the moment
With such gold - that gilds the mind. All is blent,
Enlightened, overwhelmed - as daylight tracks

The dazzle of a star - at summer's zenith.
Matins, none, and vespers, are subsumed
As swallows burn their throats and temper blue
And heat: becomes a psalm - a benediction.

THE BATTLE OF ASHINGDON. (For the Unborn)

St Nicholas surmounts this ancient hill
Where old Canute contrived to gain a crown
And England's heart. Now the Kentish ragstone
Soaks the rain that comes in slants from eastern
Cold domains - and chills the doves. To understand
The processes of time when Ironsides
Encamped across the plains is more than minds
Can manage in this place when all the land
Is plotted, pieced, and ploughed. The light decrees
A stasis in the tides as blood and bone
Remembered - haunt the air - and bruise the clouds.
St Nicholas would have another will

When fathers lost their children with their lives
In fields of death. The patron saint of Christmas
Watches still as fieldfares plunder hawthorn
And the mud - is turned to gore. You cannot
Enter heaven - so it's said - unless
A child ravishes your soul and calms
Your breath. Peace and plenty? Where now the psalms?
The poetry of love? The festival
Is coming - Advent dawns - but this dark spot
Is tainted by the past. Who - yes who - is born?
Not it seems descendants through the mist
Of ghostly prows: and battle-shields - and silence.

MIGRATIONS

The geese - fly over: their clanking chains
And hellish autumn voices arrange

The leaves like embers in a fire
And chill the air. No-one can now aspire

As frost brings down the stars on grass and thorn
And summer ends as winter's dark is dawning

Beside the lake. The robin sings its song
And all that once were rights are now the wrongs

Of cold November's grey, indifferent breath.
This is the time of questions - time of test:

The veil is thin - the memory condensed
To phantom shapes and those relentless

Thoughts - that freeze the heart. The Canadas
Slide down a chute of light where even landing

Doubles and dissolves in deep reflections.
Here is the place, the meaning, and the context

Where love is lost and hope can only drown
Amongst the leaves. Gold's an uncanny shroud

As sacred trees are silently disrobed
And thoughts of life are clouded by the snows

That haunt the mind. Where - have the swallows gone:
A transmigration - death - or deep in ponds -

When all that's left is squandered and denuded
And only ice: illuminates - the truth?

'BEEING'

A complex thing a flower: style
And stigma - pollen and anthers. The bees
Know without knowing - they have no guile

Where life's concerned. For them - no complexities:
Discovery - entrance and exit -
Their employ is done unknowingly.

Quid pro quo is all of nature's text
And they will know the letter and the law
Without a thought. For us - perplexity:

We need to know the measurement of doors
Where they just enter in and take their fill
Of light and nectar. Would - that we were less sure:

Were less obsessed with matter and its ills
And more concerned to feel - than be alarmed.
The choice is in the mind - or of the will -

When all the world would offer us a psalm
Instead of prose. The bee - just hovers:
Just hangs there - like a talisman - a charm -

When you and I would filch each hive like robbers
And gorge - and swill. The bee - knows not - the seed:
But it will procreate - without the bother -

That we attach to hormones and to genes.
The helix spirals deeper through our minds
But are the depths: ascendant - or diseased?

A WORD ABOUT SNOW

What to say about snow: only whiteness -
No colour - no shape - just uniformity.
This page started out as winter: light
Without the Word - cold and meaningless. Form -
What is it? Bird-tracks through the woods? Starlight
In the darkness? A poem must be born:

Must condense like air - precipitate
On paper. A blackbird moves from branch
To branch: a contrast - a chance that's taken
Unawares. Black on white - the newly blanched
Encoded. Ice: once water - once air - partakes
Of the mystery. The substance-less advances:

Crystals configure - light solidifies.
There's not much left to say - the weather's
Said it all. It's there in the leaden skies -
The silent earth. The blackbird's feathers
Shake and down the air a frozen thought - replies.
Let's finish this - let's finish this together.

The sunlight finds a rift in all this grey
And you and I must travel to the cause
Of our cold breath. Yes - water drips - today:
Evaporates - and once again is nought.
The blackbird leaves his perch and flies away
And we are left: to light - without a clause.

OPTICAL

How often have I peered into this river:
Scried the depths for answers or ideas
Where light is like a mirror as it quivers
And time - stands still. Strange how the passing years
Can meet and merge when images deliver
Up their ghosts - and all is one. I do not fear

The past - nor yet the future - when I assess
Inverted trees or flowers that breathe
The deep reflections of themselves. I guess
It's just a dream. An illusion: something seen
But not quite there - a coalescing
Vision of a thought of all that's been

And all that's yet to happen. The fish move through
The clouds - invade the sun: What can I say
When nothing here is real - when depths of blue
Are just a nether sky and daylight
Is divided through the glass? Beauty - truth -
Who knows? I see no point in praying:

Life is itself a prayer - to be is enough
I'm sure - what else is needed? Is that me
Who's looking back? Am I just a bluff -
A semblance - an idea? Someone who's free -
Or like a fly in amber? I see the thrush:
Its double song is now a full reprise

Where sound and sight inhabit two known worlds
That I - don't know. The lily floats a flower
And water droplets shimmer as if pearls
On every petal. A dream - some timeless hour?
It matters not as galaxies unfurl
And rainbows make a falsehood out of showers.

'BLACKTHORN WINTER'

Take heart - the spring is dawning:
The daffodil's a clarion
Of love - and light is born.
There are no frozen barriers -
The frost has lost its form
And hope's dishevelled sparrows

Build their nests. Each lark has lifted:
Ascendancy has songs
Beyond the mind - and heaven's gift
Is closer to belonging
Than you could know. The swifts
Are almost here and winter's wrongs

Are coming to an end. This cuckoo's
Double note defies all death
When April reaches blueness
And the sky - is nature's message.
The blackthorn knows the truth:
There'll be no snow - no frost to test

The blood - the weather's warming vow
Will hatch the egg - will feed the thrush.
Take heart - the spring is now:
The foliage is rushing
To comply and lofted clouds
Are whiter than the doves.

The crocus opens wide its golden gape
And sunlight: quells its hunger - and assuages.

CONVERSING WITH SNOWDROPS

The snowdrops are late this year: Just one
Or two, despairing at the lack of light -
Hanging their heavy heads. Why has the sun
Deserted us? Why is the season's tide
So full at ebb? Come - spring: bring us the sight
Of flowers - the sound of birds, become

Our hopes, our dreams, our aspirations - take
Us to the summerlands of love. Snowdrops -
Why do you hang your heads? The stormcock breaks
The silence with a wish, and buds that show
Embolden bush and tree. The emotions
Are but latent - always there: a thought will make

The difference, if you dare - will take you
To the swallow and the swift, where time
Is air enlightened by their wings, and blue
The compensation of belief. Sunshine
In the mind is all you need to prime
Your warmest thoughts: to take you to the truth

Within the rose - within the dove. Love will
Lift your heads: will melt the frost, the snow,
And your cold hearts. Time will be fulfilled:
The darkness of the earth - you have outgrown -
So take your chances now when light is slow
And listen for the larks above the hills.

GOLD RUSH

The crocus stakes a claim: mines its own
Gold - assays the sun. A chaffinch riddles
Air with each sung note - and ingots grow
As celandine increases. Let's bid
For all this treasure: offer more than prose
For each grown leaf - for every song. Let's rid

Ourselves of winter with a prayer - let's proffer
Up our earnestness for light and bless the sun
For being not - pyrites. What once was loss
Is now our living gain where death becomes
A memory - all that's past - and profit
Is the pearl in every bud. Soon the plum,

The cherry, and the pear, will toss their perfect
Blossoms to the wind, as if a care
Were something to deny when birdsong
Primes the blood in every heart. Despair's
An alter image of the light: a worthless
Thought duality decrees when prayer

Proposes oneness - and the rose. Listen:
The lark composes love with its sweet bill
And music gilds the heavens with a kiss.
Each primrose bites a nugget on the hills
As cuckoos delve to double notes of bliss
And swell the purse: with promises - fulfilled.

LARKSONG AND LEAF-FALL

The same things say it all: the scarlet leaves
That fade and fall through mist, when autumn talks
Of endings - and the sun - is less believed
Than rooks across the fields. These mushroom stalks
Are tonsured - like the monks - who once conceived
In cloisters of the mind - that those who walked

Through shadows came to light and hope was made
Incarnate in the stars. This dark denuded
Land is far from barren: The seeds parade
Their purpose under ice and even truth
Is blessed within the bud. I'm not afraid -
At least - not always: the solstice proves

That darkness cannot last and soon enough
The snowdrops will appear to fill my heart
With promise - and with faith. I hear the thrush,
The blackbird, and the wren, and all that's past
Prepares me for the rose - and thoughts of love.
I'm not alone, though timelessness is vast,

And my amens - though earnest - can't quite still
The dirge of doves. The summerlands must come:
Must lift the lark above this misted hill
Where blue will be begotten - and the sun -
Will shine within a monstrance that reveals
A seraph's elevation: death - undone.

WOODLAND RIDE

There are angels in the trees:
I've seen their golden wings
  When autumn comes
  And silks and mist
Diaphanous as dreams
    Gild every eye.
Heaven? Yes - believe:
    The seraphim
- Descended from the sun -
  Have come to kiss
The stratas - and the seams -
  In this grey ride.

The toadstools have conceived:
I have heard the robin sing
When he becomes
The king of this dank tryst
  And gleams
   - Like fire.
Earth - is yet - deceived:
These scarlet things
  Are fungal
  - Don't resist -
The toxins have their shamanistic schemes
And you will know of frost as love's own pyre
  Amongst the leaves.

THE WAY IT IS

It's the way it is:
The sun appears to rise
But it doesn't -
The moon shines
Yet it has no light.
The daffodil is everything
But yellow
And air's invisibility
Turns to mist.
I like illusions:
The sky's blue pretence -
The solidity of images in water.
When I see the acorn
Can I see the oak?
The blackbird sings
But sound is just an echo -
A vibration.
Take this stone:
Drop it on your foot -
Is the stone real?
Is the pain a feeling?
Particles, energy, consciousness:
Who knows?
Some stars are there
Yet they are not -
Some are not
And yet they are!
Whatever, they cook our bones:
Make water for the tides -
Orchestrate the curlew's
Haunted music.
It's the way it is -
Or isn't:
When you observe - you create -
When you close your eyes
The dream: gestates - in darkness.

NEW YEAR'S DAY

The streetlamps dazzle through the winter trees:
A million droplets of enlightened silver
Shimmer with the stuff of galaxies
As a robin - is awoken - and delivers

Its doleful song. This is how it dawns
This damp New Year as light and dark
Debate their proper place and something's born -
Though what - we are not sure. Janus marks

The season - double faced - that we might see
The future and the past - as we still live.
Yet now is all we have - and memory -
To praise - or curse - the taker and the giver

Of our desires. The droplets - fail and form:
And down the drizzled air night's aftermath
Anoints the solemn meaning of the paths
With moistened thoughts: turned wistful - like the morning.

BLACKBIRD AND BLOSSOM

Dark night of the soul - what is it? Overcoming
Separateness - facing extinction
Of the self? The unconscious is sunless -
Or is it? Without the stars it's winter:

Always winter. Can one ever breakdown
In selflessness? What is the endless thought
That's craving form? Are heaven's open gates
The way to hell? The blackbird is a sport -

And so are we: and yet it sings - and singing
Moves our hearts; when it itself would only
Find a mate - or feed its brood. Belonging:
Is it instinct? Sense without thinking? A dream

Without temporal meaning? The blackbird
Is in the blossom: its lyric orchestrates
My being where black and white's a church
That I believe - despite survival. Take

Heed of the light this spring: out of the darkest
Depths the word is born and love's illumination
Will return - like swifts and swallows. Laugh
With the yaffle and the cuckoo: the blue

You see - in essence - is the sky but there
Is more to this than doves or demons
When selfhood dies. What need have you of prayer?
The blossom falls in drifts across the breeze

But soon the fruits will burden every branch
And quench the tongue: as summertime - advances.

HADLEIGH RAY

The slipway is half submerged: slopes into
The cold, grey creek - as if to make submission
To the moon whose gravity and day-assuming
Skull - is framed in blue. There is a misted

Ambience that chills as curlews call
Their solitary notes and ghosted
Music shivers with the tide. The old seawall
Curves towards the castle from the coast

Where ancient heights are grazed or sown with wheat
And thoughts of spring return again to winter.
There are a few new shoots - a few new leaves:
But mostly there are geese on spectral wings

Who fail to set their bearing for the north
And summer's tundra. A shelduck laughs:
An eerie sound from some unearthly source
That takes the mind through fathoms to the past

On this bleak shore. A Viking longship draws
Its shallow draught towards a Saxon inlet
In the marsh where timbers rot and nets are stored
Away - and all is silence. I am perplexed:

Where are the warriors - the fishermen -
The farmers? Is this time or timelessness?
A curlew sounds its isolate amen
As April's early tide begins to rise

Across the flats. What century is this?
The crows - that could be ravens - taunt the gulls
As wooden craft - reflected - lift and list
And ghastly lights: illuminate - their hulls.

TURNSTONES (Southend-on-Sea, Essex)

The turnstones are becoming tame: they strut
Their coastal stuff away from the sea's edge -
Are stop and start along the promenade
As if people had ceased to exist -
Had dematerialised. Some are sprung
Like arrows across the road: fletched in black
And white - homing in on bread - attractions
Offered and gratefully received. The sun
Dazzles and defines: picks them out as they drift
Across the seawall - settle and wander
In frenetic circles. Their wings are wedges:
They open and close - flap and stutter -

Are driven in by the wind - to stop
The gaps in darkness - gaps in light.
Winter visitors: inverse trippers basking
In fog and frost - alluvial storms - slants
Of occasional sunlight. Geese and ducks
Bob on the leaden waters: the turnstones
Look on - are waiting for the tidal zone -
Where shoals and mud revalidate their luck
With worms and molluscs. Is it choice or chance?
Like us they are a product of the stars
Who feed - or fail to navigate their lives
As turning tides: and phases - chart, our options.

REFLECTIONS - SUGAR MILL COTTAGES
(Hoe Mill - Essex)

These cottages by the canal: the old
Mill worker's dwellings - where time is seen
In sepia and all the reeds are golden
In the sun - this cold December. Between

The wooden footbridge and the bend as ghostly
Horses tow their heavy loads and barges
Blend their spectral images: I know
Beyond all reason - something other - where past

Perceptions waver in the depths and lives
That were, are now - perhaps forever -
In my chill vision. These frosted skies
Are more than winter's roof - more than weather:

They are it seems as nebulous as truth
Where atmosphere and essence meld and merge
And chains of clanking geese are part assumed
Within the mirror's: mystery - unworded.

DREAMS OF FISH AND OTHER FORMS

When I was young and happy - I remember -
The willow pond, the willows, and the fish:
The crucian carp, the sticklebacks, and roach
That found me by the crowsfoot and the lilies
In my heart's spring. Time I know is passing:
But even now the thought of old excitements

Refresh my mind. There are it seems excitements
That return when age itself remembers
And relives - the ancient dream. What's passing -
Is not passing: all those golden fish
Are swimming still between the open lilies
And the sun. The sticklebacks and roach

Sink through the clouds: so many silver roach
Amongst the weeds that even now excitements
Are the same - not just a dream. Those lilies
Are no myth - they still exist: remember
Them - remember if you can how all life's fish
Are tangible in time - that is not passing.

Believe me - just relax: What's passing
Are the aspects of a thought - a thought of roach,
The crowsfoot, and the willows: eternal fish,
Eternal plants, and trees. Excitements -
Yes - excitements - are the same: remember
And relive - revivify: the lilies

Open wide their golden cups - yes lilies
Hold the demoiselles of summer. In passing
I should say - you should not think: remember
In a thoughtless sort of way and rising roach
Concentric in the mind will find excitements
Widening in waves. They're only fish

You say: believe me they are more than fish
To me - the crowsfoot and the lilies -
Sticklebacks - are life's and love's excitements
Given form when I who pass - not passing -
Hold the dream. My life is lived for roach:
I love them now as much as I remember

Those former fish that live - and are not passing.
Subconscious lilies hold their shoals of roach
And all excitements merge - as I remember.

ALL IS NOW

Time and tide they are not passing
All is now - of that I'm sure;
The cuckoo chimes - the skylark soars -
The yaffle drills or else it's laughing
When the light itself advancing
Tells a lie - not nature's law.
Time and tide they are not passing
All is now - of that I'm sure -
Who in Lent would suffer fasting
Here at heaven's open door?
Without a doubt the blackbird's score
Lifts the heart to where the stars sing -
Time and tide they are not passing
All is now - of that I'm sure.

I SEE THE SNOW

I see the snow that's falling in your heart
And I am loathe to leave you here alone
In this cold place. I would that you could ask:
When I see you - so frigid - flesh and bone

My wish is that my love could hear you moan
With warm desire. Your eyes - reflect the past:
There - in icy depths - that I'd disown
I see the snow that's falling in your heart

And in these woods. The crystals fall - like stars -
But your estate is frozen - un-atoned:
I love you yet I fear your blameless glance
And I am loathe to leave you here alone

To fret and freeze. I wish that you'd condone
My former sins: forgive the passing
Aspect of my faults and thaw the pulse of stone
In this cold place. I would that you could ask -

Could ask me to be penitent - not dark:
Though whiteness sheds its tenor and its tone
As winter melts and sunlight bares the grass
When I see you - so frigid - flesh and bone -
        I see the snow.

ANOTHER LIGHT

There is another light - another sun:
A universe illumined by a word
That no-one speaks and no-one understands
Save those in love. The nightingale affirms

This simple truth when some would say absurdly
That it's dumb - to passion's voice. The tongue
May touch the palate and the teeth - yet be unheard:
There is another light - another sun -

Where silences are subtle and succumb
To other stars. Remember that lone bird
That sings aloud when night cannot expunge
A universe - illumined by a word

That lights the heart. A madrigal - a verse -
Is all you need to hear the peerless wisdom
Of the doves. Some say - that time is terse:
That no-one speaks and no-one understands

The silent side of sentiments unsung
In this dark world. Be not disturbed:
Be not concerned by words that all would shun
Save those in love. The nightingale - affirms -
                    another light.

SILENCES AND SOUND

The leaves turn: yellow and red, gold and brown.
There is a sadness hereabouts: the robin's
Autumn song is tenuous: a vow,
Like gossamer, like frost. Think of winter
And you'll know the sound I mean: a plough
Through dark earth, seagulls crying, scintillations
Of ice, freezing fog. Where now the songs of spring?
The leaves sidle in silence: drift and fall,

Fathom and float. Not here the lofted call
Of larks in blue: only the ringing
Strands of frosted silk; tension, glitterings.
Mist and attendant memory, whispers, shrouds:
The snowdrops are buried deep; not a hint
Of anything, only fog, woodsmoke. Brown
Leaves and gold, red and yellow, splinters
Of ice: toadstools lift their tonsures, resound

In the silence, like faith. Funereal
The robin's song - its threnody. Singing
Without solace, a dirge, notes that spin
Their radial geometries. What appals
More than this? Snowfall? Slants of rain? Clouds?
Diagonals of light, coruscate, shimmer:
The robin's song is thinner than it sounds
And down the air, the silences, impinge.

AS ABOVE

We talk of life, of love, and inner light
As if our hope was centred on the stars
And fuelled by fire. In truth, it is the night
And not the moon that holds us in its arms
With thoughts of death when we would touch the heights
And iridize, and even shine. Don't ask
The silent galaxies to speak: they cannot
Hear your questions, even care, when language

Constellates on thoughts of loss. The spirit's need
Is silence, and the frost: when winter
Fills the heavens with Orion and the Pleiades
Are muted; far and cold. We need not sing,
There's music in the spheres: our soul's own dream
Can resonate, like ice, that's tinkling
With its crystal serenades. Life's madrigals
Can freeze, like this night's fog, but overall

The density of air that turns our breath
To ghosts, as we still live, cannot declare
Our blood is once, for all; a certain death.
Just look above, forget the realms of prayer:
There's no eternal need of time or text,
Of hope, or life, or love, or yet despair,
Your inner light is outer, like our star,
And what you are, is counter, to the darkness.

FIELDS OF VISION (The Battle of Assundune - 1016)

There is more down this lane than nature:
There is time and timelessness, blackberry
Preserves, elderberry wine, pictures

Of the past in fermentation. There are tracks
between the fields; ways between wheat
Winding towards the Crouch, a battlefield

Long-buried under pasture. Victory
Or defeat; what matters? There is verdure,
Larksong; salt-laden tides, springs and neaps.

The cognoscenti of the picturesque
Ramble this way and that: consult their guides,
Maps, field-books. There is more than nature

Down this lane: more than the cabbage-whites,
Their double helices, territory.
The distended sun - corpuscular - subsides

As barn-owls quarter starlight in the east
And love's unknowing moon: ascends - decreases.

SLACK WATER

Looking out towards the pier, across the estuary,
Where Kent is misted, cut off at a distance,
I seem to sense, not time, or history,
But something else, unnamable, un-tensed.

The tides still ebb and flow, admittedly:
Gulls dip and dive, geese draw out their skeins,
Their cursive languages. Then suddenly
It stops: everything stops. A snapshot: a frame

Of infinite reference. Transparency:
All there is in aspic; simultaneous.
Positive and negative: duality,
reflections, refractions, an eternal game.

The cormorant is black; a starless mystery -
And then a wave: that crashes - sucks and sifts.

RIVER TRIPTYCH

The swan is doubled in the glass -
A question mark in darkening deeps
And though I look, and even ask,
The soundless answers sink and sleep.

A question mark in darkening deeps
Is all there is of time and truth
The soundless answers sink and sleep -
Such depths as these, they hold no proof.

Is all there is of time and truth
Just images and secrets kept?
Such depths as these, they hold no proof,
And I must drown or stay inept.

Just images and secrets kept
When I would look, and even ask,
But I must drown or stay inept
The swan is doubled in the glass.

All separateness becomes the tern
Whose parting image sinks and floats,
On air it is a thing to learn
In water but a drowning ghost.

Whose parting image sinks and floats
Where one as two remain the same -
In water but a drowning ghost
On air a white-ascendant name.

Where one as two remain the same
The thin divide is still unclear -
On air a white-ascendant name
At depth, diffuse, and turning blear.

The thin divide is still unclear -
On air it is a thing to learn
At depth, diffuse, and turning blear
As separateness becomes the tern.

The swan is doubled in the glass
Where fish just levitate and leap -
The seconds stop, before they pass,
As water shatters; clouds the deeps.

Where fish just levitate and leap
Concentric circles take their place
As water shatters; clouds the deeps,
Obliterates the staring face.

Concentric circles take their place
When vision's mirror holds the gloom -
Obliterates the staring face
With prophecies of certain doom.

When vision's mirror holds the gloom
The seconds stop, before they pass -
With prophecies of certain doom
The swan is doubled in the glass.

HEAVEN AND HELL

The river is clear and calm:
Almost as if it didn't exist -
An indivisible transparency.

A shoal of roach are suspended -
Not in mid-water, but in mid-air.

The cabbage weeds are trees:
Trees in a deep abyss
With me between them

Inhaling their oxygen - their purpose.
The loosestrife are purple torches:

Flames in the depths of Hades;
Lighting the way to nowhere -
To nothingness. I believe in pike:

Ariel torpedoes - striped for the hidden
Moment - the final attack - apocalypse.

Can they savage a reflection:
Tear the illusion apart -
Where nothing is and nothing happens

Save for the dream's intangibility -
The imaginary depths? Clear and calm:

I will walk into the river -
Hover like a kestrel - or an angel.
The roach are cherubim and seraphim:

The pike - an image of Lucifer -
Fallen: fathomless - irrefutable.

THE BURE MARSHES (Norfolk)

Where do I go from here: the lane ends
At the reeds and the marshes and all there
Is is sky and clouds and sunlight. I tend
To think too much: I could listen instead
To the warblers, take notice of the air's
Unnamable fragrance, see the sparkling
Coruscations on the dyke. But my head
Is always with the sky: the endless, vast,

Infinity of blue that overarches
Everything there is and leaves the dead
To silence under skylarks. Why do I ask
Such questions? The swallows are a prayer
Across the grasses but I am led
Forever by my eyes towards the spent
Existence of a mill that holds despair
In weeds and crumbled brick. If I could sense -

Just sense in something other: some recompense -
Some meanings - something else; that would repair
The emptiness of fields, the pointless tense
Of clouds that form and fade, the living red
Of poppies - slowly wilting. But I - just stare:
At night this disappears - save for the stars -
And all there is are dreams that dare to tread
Beyond the owls: the pipistrelles - and darkness.

REPRISE
('The wise thrush sings its song twice over': Robert Browning)

The thrush repeats its winter song
From ever dank and leafless trees
As if in essence it belongs
To rain and other minor keys.

From ever dank and leafless trees
The thrush assails the darkening gates
Of rain and other minor keys -
Where sadness sighs so much of late

The thrush assails the darkening gates
And rattles off its bright reprise.
Where sadness sighs so much of late
The thrush outpours its urgent pleas

And rattles off its bright reprise
As if in essence it belongs.
The thrush outpours its urgent pleas
And thus repeats its winter song.

THE SEASON BURNS

The season burns when sunlight moves the doves
To summer sounds and syllables of heat
Amongst the leaves. What is there but enough
In our warm hearts when love repeats

Its meaning in a song and time's conceit
Is nothing but a drone? Instinct is the sun:
Are you - not here - contented and complete?
The season burns when sunlight moves the doves

And cabbage-whites and commas float above
Like careless thoughts - unreasoned and replete -
As are the bees. The threnody succumbs
To summer sounds and syllables of heat

As collared-doves and turtles still the breeze
And thermals rise on spirals made of dust
To taint the rose and whisper - like defeat -
Amongst the leaves. What is there but enough?

The commas' wings - though comparable with rust -
Are living yet in light with such belief
That sears the mind. You cannot chill the blood
In our warm hearts: when love - repeats
                              the season - as it burns.

STARGAZING

I think of you when I am here alone
And love again is woken in my heart
And in my mind. There's more than flesh and bone:
The spirit knows its semblance in the stars

And though the soundless universe is vast
I feel you close. Perhaps we touch a zone
That knows all zones. Whatever - truth - or mask:
I think of you when I am here alone

And particles of passion - once unknown -
Just come to pass. I see beyond Polaris:
When I recall your tenor and your tone
And love again is woken in my heart

And in my soul. Time's - not in the past:
Eternally the moment turns to stone -
A lapidary vision in the dark
And in my mind. There's more than flesh and bone:

The Pleiades, Orion, and the Swan
Were once a thoughtless thought - a question asked:
But now they manifest the perfect koan -
The spirit knows its semblance in the stars.

You are here unending - heaven's arc:
Though we're apart togetherness has grown
Molecular, and mute, and unsurpassed.
Believe me now when silence gilds the moon -
                          I think of you.

PERHAPS I'M WRONG

Perhaps I'm wrong - but the snowdrops
Speak of spring and thoughts of frost
Have liquefied in light on this
Warm day. Freezing fogs and mist
Are now elsewhere as my heart's clock

Strikes noon - and blackbirds sing - and loss
Is lightened. What is the cost
Of hope, of faith, of mystery?
                    Perhaps I'm wrong

But I am sure that snowdrops can move rock:
Can lift their whispering heads and mock
The moon - with fired whiteness. Bliss -
Who knows? Winter? Valediction?
Whatever - something's greener - even moss -
                    Perhaps I'm wrong.

PASSING IMAGES

From the bridge at Baddow I peer
Into the depths: how clear
The water seems - my image doubles
In the deeps as swallows trouble
Their own reflections with wings that veer

And shatter surfaces. What's here
To be done in summer? The weir
Whispers over sills and bubbles
Proliferate: loosestrife and lilies appear
                    From the bridge at Baddow.

The fields are harvested: turned blear
In the August haze - austere -
Yet golden. Look at the stubble:
There too the swallows veer - over the rubble
Of another season - another year -
                    From the bridge at Baddow.

THE TRAGEDY OF LOVE

We are one - according to tradition:
As the spectrum turns to whiteness, we, as male
And female are indivisible. Listen:
The dove's song and the dove curtail

All thoughts of separateness - unity
Is summer and the heat. But you and I
Have our own ideas: the illusion
Keeps us apart - is as arbitrary as time.

I look into your eyes - hold your hand -
But Sirius turns to ice: holds winter
In this frozen, summer moment. Understand
What you will: to know is not to integrate -

To experience. Behold the collared-doves:
It is not love that fuels their soft syllabics -
Only the need to parley with the sun;
Instinctive: unalloyed - and somehow, tragic.

SKYLARKS AND CUMULI

If you like the sun - and summer -
Remember the lark and the dove
Make good companions. That the lark
Will lift his song towards the stars
Although they are not visible - undone -

In depths of blue. If there is love
In your definitions, if suchness
Is the scent of the rose - then laugh -
                    If you like the sun.

But if sadness is the honeysuckle:
Heat a monotonous dirge - overcoming
Levity - then remember the past
Is not the past - that now is the lark
Climbing till the cumuli succumb -
                      If you like the sun.

THE SHIVERING STARS

How can you see in the shivering stars
The pulse and creation of love?
Watching Orion, the Swan, and Polaris
What can you see in the shivering stars?
How do you know that the warmth of the heart
Comes from a region so cold and afar?
How can you see in the shivering stars
The pulse and creation of love?

REASONABLE THINGS

Winter comes - spring follows - such is the way
        Of reasonable things.
The sea has tides - the moon its phases:
Winter comes - spring follows - such is the way
Of reasonable things. Love has its day,
Or so it's said - the bee its delirious daisies:
Winter comes - spring follows - such is the way
        Of reasonable things.

THE SNOW FALLS

The snow falls - straight down in continuous lines -
A geometry of cold, condensing light.
There is silence and the senselessness of time
While the snow falls - straight down in continuous lines:
The vaulted trees - are birdless - yet sublime
As whiteness arcs, dislodges, or defines.
The snow falls - straight down in continuous lines -
A geometry of cold, condensing light.

THE WHISPERING SWANS

Are you alone by the edge of the lake
Watching the whispering swans?
Lover of light and the image you make
Are you alone by the edge of the lake?
Where the swallows that glance are a paean of praise
And reflections are hard to forsake,
Are you alone by the edge of the lake
Watching the whispering swans?

FALLING LEAVES

The robin sings its melancholy song
And love - is somewhere else:
Winter comes towards us with its wrongs
And the robin sings its melancholy song.
How could we - here in autumn - just belong
When leaves are lamentations - golden throngs?
The robin sings its melancholy song
And love - is somewhere else.

THE TROUBLE WAS HE BATTLED WITH THE STARS

The trouble was he battled with the stars:
Could see no point in living - save the night -
Where love was lost - eternally - to darkness.

Orion as the hunter - and Polaris -
Invested him with images of light:
The trouble was he battled with the stars

And lost his soul. And yet - he had a heart:
But he could not retrieve it from the heights
Where love was lost - eternally - to darkness.

He separated - present and the past -
And couldn't see the moment was just right:
The trouble was he battled with the stars

Yet failed to shine. He only knew disaster:
Could see no iridescence - no delight -
The trouble was he battled with the stars
Where love was lost - eternally - to darkness.

SUMMER RAIN (for Edward Thomas and Alice Meynell)

The rain - it never stops: continuous
And drenching - filling drains - for three whole days
It's travelled down the leaves and drowned the things
Of summer with its song. The flower sprays

Are silent - dripping wet: as doves and thrushes
Hunch amongst the trees and ponds repeat
The lyrical refrain of June's unjust
Interment of the rose. Light and heat

Are languishing elsewhere and nothing sings
Of summer - sings of love: the only phrase
Or cadence is the dirge of hampered wings
And damp undelving bees. The orchard ways

Are puddled underfoot and apples gush
With droplets - clear cascades - of silvered green.
A blackbird tries his music in the hush
But even he - dishevelled and demeaned -

Cannot encourage summer to relent
When Queen-Anne's-lace is colourless and cold
And all is blent with loss and lamentations.
The evening comes without a hint of gold

As one uncertain moth picks up the scent
Of moonless stocks: and pluvial - momentum.

'CAN SPRING BE FAR BEHIND'
(For P B Shelley and Thomas Hardy)

The stormcock sings: its darkling notes enlighten
Winter skies - and warm the heart. 'Can spring
Be far behind'? The snowdrops turn from night
Into the day - and whiteness whispers. Things

Are on the move: the collared-doves drop
Syllables of sound that raise the sap
In elder and my veins as thoughts of frost
Dissolve and deliquesce and some perhaps

Unfolds - a golden flower. See now -
Beside this river: the celandine that parley
With the sun - are certainties - are vows
Like bright doubloons - that offer wealth and bask

In thoughts of May. Winter - loses strength:
The chaffinch knaps its flint - and sudden sparks -
Stream out their notes in lines of summer's length
Where waters thaw and flow - as is their task -

While yet the darkling thrush uplifts his song
And we are warmed: with wisdom - and belonging.

THE SAXON SHORE

Not picturesque admittedly: Barling
Magna borders on the tides with landfill
Sites and aggregates unearthed and farmer's
Fields laid flat to far horizons. Understand:

The past is yet the present - this Norman church
Has seen the ebb and flow of many lives
From fishermen to peasants, where now the birds -
The robin and the wren - are striving

With the weather - known as time. Remember
As the season slowly turns and neaps
And springs bring snow beneath the moon - that semblance
Comes in many disparate forms - and dreams

Have meaning. The whooper swans find blades of winter
Wheat and fuel the thought's transmission into
Light - from some dark word. These geese have wings -
These cottages have smoke: and both diffuse

In evanescent skeins into the skies.
I walk between the hawthorn and the scrub
Towards the haunts of smugglers - and their rum -
Where time on time inverts and overlies

As ghostly prows bring dragons to the shores
And ravens fly: with eyes - attuned to glory.

A DALLIANCE WITH RAINBOWS

There's evidence of sunshine in my heart
As blackbirds sing and crocuses aspire
Towards the light. The celandine are stars
In atmosphere: golden - solar fires

Of the spring that bring to earth the galaxies
Of night - transformed with blossom. Desire
Is delivered without cost as sunlight tracks
An ever higher arc and love inspires

Dalliance with rainbows. The adder basks
And warms its winter blood as if the fact
Of venom were denied and it would ask
A truce - with life and death. Hope - reacts:

Is taken ever skyward with the lark
To touch the edge of cumuli and sapphire -
Where breath and southern airs belie the dark
And swallows: create music - on the wires.

ST PETER'S CHAPEL

What do you meet here: here at the sea's edge,
The cold, grey, northern sea? Salt winds,
Seagulls, geese? Susurrations through the sedge,
Occasional sunlight; larksong? Sinners

Know this place: Bradwell-juxta-Mare, where St Cedd
Landed, built his chapel from the ruins
Of a Roman fort, prayed for heathens, bled
For his faith. So many different truths:

Myths, meanings, allegories. What's said
May be believed: Stone on stone the chapel
Was erected; stones for the heart, the head;
Stones for God, stones for man; stones. Perhaps

It all made sense, still does: souls must be fed,
Spirits lifted. The sun breaks through the clouds:
A dozen larks ascend, and thoughts, like lead
Rise on enlightened wings and make their vows

To sunlight's silver monstrance. Poppies bleed red:
Summer wine, fermenting in the wheat,
The body's blood, the living and the dead,
Where tides of light are shimmering in heat.

The season flows to autumn; then it ebbs,
And swallows leave: and geese - fly overhead.

A MAN IN THE PARK

He found his way to the park. Sat down
On a bench. Looked up at the stars.
The night was frosty. Lights from town

Left him in a black hole: the past,
Memory, nothing else. Sounds
Of distant traffic haunted the cast

Of his mind, his fix on meaning. Around
Him, the air condensed its silences:
Cold, sharp, icy. A tissue of cloud

Scuffed at the moon's fist quarter. Tense
Was somewhere else: there with the barking
Dog, the scrape of a shovel, a sense

Of coal hitting the bucket - darkness.
The stars seemed old, infinitely
Old. Everything - endless and vast:

Colder than ice, colder than winter.
What was it he remembered:
Happier times, youthfulness, a hint

Of a pure belief, December
Personified? An aircraft droned:
Lights flickering, immemorial embers.

The moon darkened, it started to snow -
His breath was ghosted: transient – unknowing.

SIRIUS SINGING

Take, for instance, July: the Dog Star rises
With the sun and the diminutive wren
Enlarges its summer song. The sky
Is Wedgwood blue and the light that bends

Around the earth invests the present time
With memories and meanings - fired -
Like early porcelain. What is this thought
That settles on the rose: this causeless

Cause reflected in the dew that scents
The mind with mystery and wonder?
We think we choose - but do we? Moments,
Sequences; ideas of purpose: the sun's

Irrepressible heat, languishes - mingles
With the doves' syllabics - warms the illusion.
Colour turns to whiteness - like syringa,
And the spectral wren: illuminates - a truth.